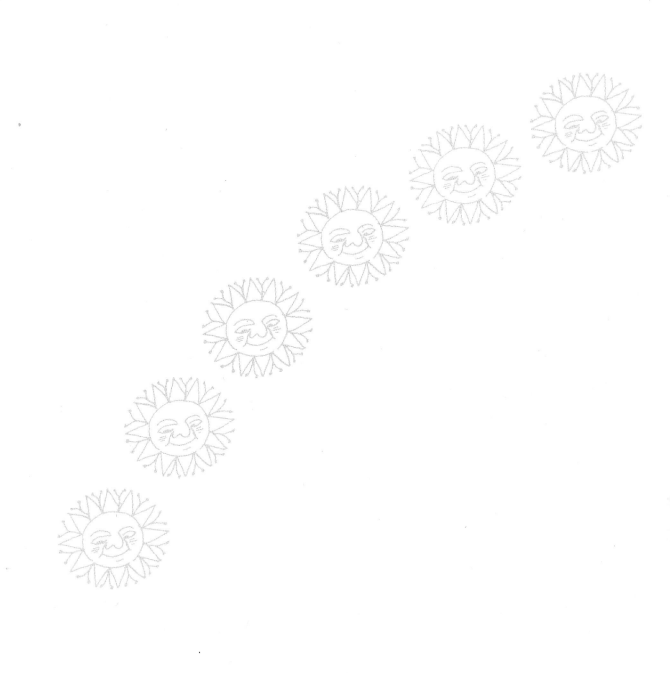

greenhousing
for purple thumbs

dx fenten

drawings by maggie baylis
architectural drawings by roy killeen

101 productions
san francisco

Printed and bound in the United States of America.

Distributed to the book trade in the United States
by Charles Scribner's Sons, New York, and in Canada
by Van Nostrand Reinhold Ltd., Toronto

Published by 101 Productions
834 Mission Street
San Francisco, California 94103

Library of Congress Cataloging in Publication Data

Fenten, DX
    Greenhousing for purple thumbs.

    Includes index.
    1. Greenhouse management.   I. Title.
SB415.F38   635'.04'4   76-26055
ISBN O-89286-105-3
ISBN O-89286-104-5 pbk.

contents

why garden under glass?

Outside there's snow or sleet or driving, freezing rain. Traffic is snarled to a standstill, tempers are short and nature has found a way to short-circuit humanity. The television set advises us to "get away from it all." In more and more places around the world and especially in North America, people are finding a new and exciting way and place to "get away from it all."

A greenhouse owner in the Northeast who has been gardening under glass for a bit more than a year reports: "I can have fresh strawberries in December (without paying a dollar a box), and fresh tomatoes all year long. I can have tropical plants blooming at the peak of their beautiful perfection in my home whenever I want them to bloom. You just can't beat it. When I'm out in my greenhouse, it's just me and my plants. The world and all its problems are far, far away."

This greenhouse gardener is a small part of the green wave that is moving steadily across the continent—a wave that is swelling bigger and bigger every year. This green wave of gardening is showing itself all over North America. Greenhouses are popping up everywhere in all sorts of sizes, shapes and designs and made from all sorts of materials.

why garden under glass?

The *Christian Science Monitor* reports, "Gardening is by far the single most popular hobby in the United States. More than 81 million Americans practice the art, and the total grows each year. Increasingly, too, gardeners are turning to the greenhouse to extend their hobby into a year 'round pastime. . . . While manufacturing in several industries has declined in recent years, greenhouse fabricators have never known it better. . . . Lord and Burnham, of Irvington, New York, the oldest and largest of the nation's greenhouse manufacturers, says business has doubled in the last five years. And the newest, Vegetable Factory, Inc., of Copiague, Long Island, says it is shipping out units almost as fast as they can be built. Then, for every factory-produced greenhouse, there are two, possibly three, homemade varieties, according to some industry 'guesstimates.'"

In the past, greenhouses, like backyard swimming pools, were for rich people. These landed gentry, with their large estates, were the only ones who could afford the luxury of a greenhouse. The original purchase price was high enough to frighten most people away from buying one, but that was only the beginning. The additional costs were staggering for the average family. Heating costs in winter, cooling costs in summer, supplies, equipment and perhaps the biggest expenditure of all—extra time. Years ago you had to watch a greenhouse constantly: adjust the heat, check the humidity, let in fresh air, water the plants and work, work, work. Not many people could afford this luxury—so much money and so much time "just for fun."

All that has changed and continues to change very rapidly. Now everyone can own and enjoy a greenhouse without spending outlandish amounts of money or time. It's all a big part of the reason for this "sudden" popularity of home greenhouses. After all these years, the parts finally fit. There are now available a whole group of factory-prefabricated units that put home greenhouses within easy reach of pocketbooks. Styles include a wide variety of freestanding units, lean-tos attached to houses and garages and small "anyone-can-afford-them" window units. To go with these new greenhouses are newly perfected

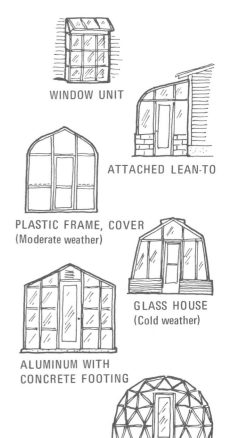

WINDOW UNIT

ATTACHED LEAN-TO

PLASTIC FRAME, COVER
(Moderate weather)

GLASS HOUSE
(Cold weather)

ALUMINUM WITH
CONCRETE FOOTING

GEODESIC, WOOD
OR ALUMINUM

7

why garden under glass?

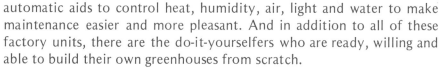

automatic aids to control heat, humidity, air, light and water to make maintenance easier and more pleasant. And in addition to all of these factory units, there are the do-it-yourselfers who are ready, willing and able to build their own greenhouses from scratch.

One Long Island greenhouse retailer who calls his establishment "a greenhouse department store" because he carries almost all brands says, "Two years ago you had to spend about $4,000 to own a greenhouse. Now it's a different story. There is great exposure in newspapers and magazines across the country of lower-priced units, some made here and some imported. People's interest is aroused. They think, 'Boy, I always wanted a greenhouse and now I can afford one.' So they start looking around and find the choice is very wide. There are many fine models available. Right now you can buy approximately the same unit as the $4,000 one with the same amount of growing space for about $800. Maybe $1,000 tops."

With the price barrier down, with more leisure time available, with less "watching" necessary, it's easy to see why so many are considering and then buying greenhouses. People who gardened outside and grew house plants indoors during the winter months, and yearned for a greenhouse of their own, as well as people who are beginning gardeners, are buying and building greenhouses. All these people, green thumbers and purple thumbers, are now gardening under glass. The reason is simple: When gardening under glass or anywhere else, there are no purple thumbs—just lots of people having fun and able to succeed at something that gives them pleasure.

Says a Midwestern woman whose entire gardening experience had been with a few philodendron bought at a local supermarket, "Greenhouse gardening is therapeutic. It's better than medicine. It's actually healing. We've all had it ... living under the cloud of constant war, political hanky-panky, and the high cost of living and breathing. The pressure on people is overwhelming. Many people, like me, are taking a new interest in the environment and especially in the things God made.

It's truly fantastic. Owning a greenhouse can really give you a new lease on life."

In the minds of some potential greenhouse owners, however, there are some reservations about the joys and freedoms of vacations and the inhibiting responsibilities of maintaining a garden or greenhouse. If we eavesdrop on an actual conversation between a Northwestern greenhouse owner and a gardener who keeps putting off a greenhouse purchase because he doesn't "want to be tied down," we'll get some answers.

"Once I buy a greenhouse and am involved with it, how much time must I put into it? Will I be tied down to it? What if I want to go away on vacation for two weeks and have a greenhouse full of plants—how can I leave it? Suppose I want to go away for a weekend, can I just pick up and go or am I tied down? Must I either take the greenhouse and the plants with me or stay home?"

"Well, for two weeks it would be necessary for you to have the same concern for the plants in the greenhouse as you would any plants you might have in your home. You would most likely arrange for someone to come in and water them. You certainly wouldn't leave them for two weeks and expect them to survive."

"You mean I could just say to a neighbor, 'Go into the greenhouse and water my plants.' Nothing more than that?"

"Nothing more than that. Keeping your plants warm is taken care of by your thermostatically controlled heater. Even if you were home, you wouldn't stand around all day staring at your heater. And, to go a step further, should it get too warm in the greenhouse, an automatic roof vent will open and allow the too-warm air out and nice fresh, cool air in. So you see, everything is now automatic—both heating and cooling. And as long as you have a friend or neighbor take care of the watering, you have nothing to worry about."

"Is that one of the reasons so many more people are buying greenhouses today, because they no longer have to become slaves to them?"

why garden under glass?

"Oh yes, there is automatic equipment available, at a reasonable price, that makes it pretty much worry-free. With the exception of watering (and you can even get automatic watering equipment if you choose to), everything else takes care of itself, whether you are there or not. You could compare it to a swimming pool. You go away and leave that for two weeks, just asking a friend or neighbor to keep up the doses of chlorine. It's the same with the greenhouse."

And, just as swimming pools are for fun, so are today's greenhouses. In the very recent past as many as four out of every five greenhouses in use were commercial ventures. Today, almost all the greenhouses being sold are for amateur gardeners who want to continue gardening all year long. That's why this "new breed" is called hobby or home greenhouses.

We who buy or build these structures are in it as a hobby. We have no great need to produce vegetables for our own tables (or for anyone else's either). We don't even have the need or desire to produce plants or flowers that can be sold at a profit. The vast majority of new greenhouse owners bought them because "it looked like great fun to be able to garden all year long."

A word, though, about vegetable and plant sales from hobby greenhouses in these times of skyrocketing prices. Though it is not the main motivation behind the purchase of a hobby greenhouse, some money can be made and some can be saved through careful, thoughtful use of these units. Many people are devoting a portion of their precious greenhouse space to growing vegetables. Those who have had their greenhouses for years and years look at vegetable growing realistically. They don't fool themselves. They don't start off saying, "I'll supply all my vegetable needs. No more high prices for me. I'll never ever have to go back to the store to buy vegetables. I can supply all my needs."

Instead, they approach the subject objectively and decide to do a limited amount of under-glass vegetable growing "to see how it goes." If it goes well, they can, and often do, expand. If it doesn't, it's back to the old drawing board for further experimentation.

why garden under glass?

Wonderfully, greenhouse gardening is more than just fun. To each owner it means something different. And, to each owner, whatever the "something" is, it's important. Talking with greenhouse owners all over the country reveals a long-lingering love with "just about the best investment we ever made." One man who grows only flowers says he loves to just look at it from his bedroom window. "Just looking at it makes me feel good. It's the best place to go for relaxation." A woman who grows everything, "especially the things everyone says you can't grow very well in a greenhouse," spends a lot of time in her lean-to model, and rarely alone. "The children beg to be allowed to go and work in the greenhouse, especially when it is miserable outside," she says. "Tempers become calm and the hours fly away. We all go out there—kids, their friends, the radio—and forget everything for a while."

SWEET POTATO VINE

Why garden under glass? Why build or buy a greenhouse? Why get involved in another responsibility? Because for as many questions like these you can raise, there are many times the number of answers, all of them sound, good, logical and positive.

• Because you will be able to garden all year long and multiply your present pleasure and relaxation manyfold.

• Because you will be able to control a small piece of nature and grow what you want to grow when you want to grow it.

• Because you will be able to see, to watch and be completely absorbed by the miracle of growth, up close, every day.

• Because you will be able to experiment and to try new things just for the sheer fun of trying them to see what will happen.

• Because the triumphs will far outnumber the disasters and the rewards will be flowers and colors and plants and fragrances and vegetables and textures that are real, that are magnificent, that are yours.

And, perhaps especially because, as one long-time greenhouse gardener says, "I'd rather buy orchids to grow in my greenhouse than pills prescribed by a doctor."

the right greenhouse for you

Are you ready? Have you decided now's the time to buy or build your very own greenhouse?

Well, now that we've gotten you all excited to get that greenhouse —wait a moment. Don't put your coat on just yet. Go into the kitchen, make a cup of coffee, sit down, relax and start thinking. Think carefully and critically: What kind of greenhouse is best for you? What kind would you like if you had your "druthers"? After daydreaming about that, come back down to earth and figure out what you can afford. What kind can you fit best on your property and—most important—do you have room for one?

Think and think again. This will be an expensive investment in both time (if you are going to build your own) and money. Why add unnecessary aggravation?

CHECK THE BOTTOM LINE

How much should *you* spend for *your* greenhouse? Do you have champagne taste and a beer budget? Are you the kind who must have the best and finest with no compromise possible? Are you interested in the cosmetic or the practical? Do you have some specific problem that will require your getting a custom-designed unit?

Investigation, through easily obtained dealer's catalogs, price lists, magazine and newspaper ads will reveal that you can buy a window greenhouse for less than $150 and freestanding, deluxe models for more than $6,000. And, of course, there are all sorts of models you can buy from one end of that price range to the other. Another solution would be to build your own, from materials costing as little as $50. Let's talk first about the factory prefabricated units and save the do-it-yourself projects for the next chapter.

The first thing to do is to start collecting as many manufacturers' catalogs as possible. This will give you the best opportunity to see and study all the available models and their prices in the quiet and privacy of your home. Here you can study, think, get your brains settled and make gentle, tentative decisions. You will usually find several models that will do what you want within the price range you want to pay.

Some will be more expensive than others, while claiming to do the same job. Why buy the more expensive model? Sometimes you don't really have a choice. If your property has unique problems, you might need a custom-built unit. Your property may require a unit that is not of standard size, and for that you will pay. If you want or need a unit that is wider than the standard 12 feet, or one that will match the decor of your house, or one that will be attached to your house through an open wall (with no door), or one that is a specific brand name, you will pay top dollar for your greenhouse. However, for these extra dollars you will not only get the perfect features for your home and property but usually a better, larger, stronger, more airtight unit as well. It may cost two to three times the price of the standard model to satisfy and solve these problems, but the solution will be there and you will have your greenhouse.

the right greenhouse

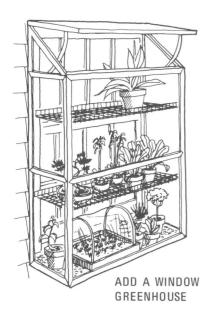

ADD A WINDOW
GREENHOUSE

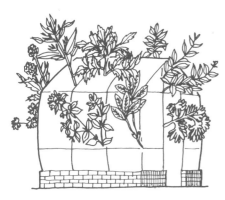

SIZE CAN BE A STUMPER

The next consideration? How big should your greenhouse be? The main complaint we've heard from greenhouse owners is that their units are too small and that they became too small too quickly, almost immediately in many cases. All owners seem to say the same thing: "I wish I had bought a bigger one."

Most of us, when trying something new, are cautious, especially when there is a sizeable investment involved. We figure to "start out small" and add another section at a later time. For some people this works out. Take the case of one Long Island woman whose interest in plants, like Topsy, just kept growing. First it was the living room window, then the kitchen window and finally the lean-to greenhouse. She started by filling her large living room window with lush plants bathed in the glow of growth lamps. It didn't take long until she expanded and put her overflow into a newly installed window unit in the kitchen. That too soon became inadequate and she bought an 8- by 12-foot lean-to greenhouse which runs the length of the den and is entered through the sliding glass doors of that room.

Another gardener bought an eight- by eight-foot freestanding unit, used it for three months, confessed to being hooked on greenhouse gardening, and added an 8- by 12-foot unit to the original. She now gardens under glass in a magnificent and beautifully cared for 8- by 20-foot greenhouse and is beginning to wonder aloud where she'll get the space she needs for the plants she wants to grow.

Despite the fact that most greenhouses are built in sections and can be enlarged, this sort of operation can be quite expensive, sometimes to the tune of double your original investment. The same-size greenhouse, bought and installed at one time, costs far less than any unit that has been expanded.

But wait, don't get us wrong. We're not suggesting that you go right out and buy a 20-, 30- or 40-foot greenhouse so you'll never be the one who ruefully realizes, "I should have made it larger; I didn't think I'd love it this much." We are suggesting that you plan carefully and select your greenhouse according to what you know you will want to grow now, what you feel you might "like to try" and what you feel you can take care of easily. Be practical, allow yourself a little dreaming and then add a little more "just because" . . . just because we know it will happen.

With automatic controls, you should be able to maintain an 8- by 10-foot unit with about one hour of work each week. If you have plenty of time and know you'll want to try many projects, start out a bit larger. As you become more and more involved and get more pleasure and more relaxation from working in the greenhouse, you'll find ways to "make more time" so you can be out there even more.

So don't start out too small. Think of growing into your greenhouse as time goes by, instead of growing out of it all too quickly.

FRAMEWORK MATERIALS: GOOD AND BETTER

Here again, the choice is yours. Will your greenhouse framework be made of aluminum, steel, redwood or some other type of wood? Will the panels of light-admitting materials be glass, fiber glass, vinyl or plastic? Each material has its advantages and disadvantages, and advocates and opponents of each have a story to tell.

Unless you don't mind almost constant maintenance of one sort or another, eliminate any thought of a wooden framework, except redwood, from your consideration. Although the other woods are much less expensive than redwood, the high humidity levels found in greenhouses cause these woods to rot and decay. As a result, they must be kept painted at all times or carefully treated with special preservatives. Because creosote, pentachlorophenol and mercury preserving compounds give off toxic fumes that will damage some plants, you will have to find a less common preservative should you decide to use a wooden frame for your greenhouse. That, plus the time involved in the actual care, make a wood frame less than ideal for most people.

Redwood is pretty, durable and a little less expensive than aluminum. According to owners who swear by the redwood structures, heat

the right greenhouse

(or cold) is transmitted many times faster through aluminum than through redwood (or any other wood). This means the wooden-frame units lose less heat and so are less expensive to operate. They are also reputed to have less chance for condensation buildup which can drip all over your plants, damaging them.

Keep in mind that, though the redwood units require very little maintenance, they should be stained, painted or otherwise treated every few years with a non-toxic material or they start to look quite shabby.

Steel is heavy, expensive and tends to rust quickly unless it has been carefully and thoroughly hot-dip galvanized. The galvanizing, or painting with red lead or aluminum, should be done after the steel has been cut to size and all holes drilled. Any area, especially the insides of holes, will start rusting when exposed to the amounts of humidity in a greenhouse. To make life with steel even more difficult, you will soon find it is incompatible with other metals, like aluminum alloy. Wherever they touch, electrolytic action breaks down the galvanizing protection and rust forms in its place.

This leaves the current favorite, aluminum alloy, which in recent years has been vastly improved and is just about the best bet for greenhouse frameworks. This material, when extruded to shape, is very strong, very lightweight (in relation to bulk), very easy to work with and very resistant to corrosion. Because of the extrusion process, the aluminum can be formed into all sorts of complicated shapes that will benefit the gardener. For example, most extruded greenhouses have drip channels (to drain off any condensation) as well as shapes that eliminate the old-fashioned putty glazing systems. This allows for simpler, less-expensive systems.

Perhaps the main reason most people buy aluminum greenhouses is that they are virtually 100 percent maintenance free. Just set them up and enjoy. No painting, treating, preserving, or anything else except hours of worry-free gardening.

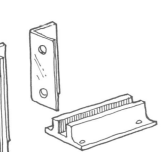

EXTRUDED ALUMINUM FORMS, FORCED THROUGH A KIND OF "COOKIE PRESS" MACHINE TO MAKE STRUCTURAL PARTS

PICKING YOUR PANELS

The selection of the material for your greenhouse panels is another one of those important decisions you must make before buying your greenhouse. The prime contenders for your affection are glass and fiber glass, with rigid plastic and plastic film bringing up the rear. And each of these has enough pros and cons to confuse everyone.

Glass is probably the most popular greenhouse panel simply because we have come to accept the fact that "glass and greenhouses go together." However, that certainly isn't a good enough reason for you to select it for your greenhouse. Glass is permanent. Put it in once and, if it's spared sonic booms, kids with BB guns or Halloween high jinks, it need never be replaced. Glass needn't be treated with preservatives or fussed over when washing. In colder climates you might think in terms of double glass for extra insulation. It is expensive, but it does save heat.

Now that you're almost convinced glass is best, here comes fiber glass. Fiber glass retains heat about four times better than glass (how about that in these days of high fuel costs?), does not shatter on impact and lasts, according to most guarantees, at least 20 years. When hit by a stone at high velocity, fiber glass will be damaged but not ruined entirely. Impact usually causes a small hole which can be patched without replacing the entire panel (which you can't do with glass).

Unfortunately, some of the less expensive fiber glass panels scratch, become dirty and then allow less light to get through to your plants. To avoid that, your best bet is a top-quality fiber glass panel that has been coated with Tedlar (PVC). This will protect it against weather and just about everything else, including a wide assortment of caustic chemicals carried by wind (especially near cities and industrial areas).

Fiber glass also has a natural shading effect, a property that's fine in the summer when there is sun to spare, but not quite so fine in winter when every bit of sun is sought and treasured.

Should you place the glass and fiber glass panels side by side it would be difficult to choose between them using cost, efficiency and maintenance as criteria. To make choosing even more difficult (or

the right greenhouse

easier, depending how you want to look at it), studies at various colleges and agricultural research centers have shown little difference between plants grown under glass or under fiber glass.

In the "you get what you pay for" category are the other greenhouse coverings. For example, high-quality sheet plastic coated with Tedlar is quite good and will last about 10 years. Uncoated sheet acrylics last for about five years and then must be steel wooled and resealed. Other plastics and plastic films are temporary and should be considered only where their low price allows you to buy a greenhouse you couldn't afford otherwise. Be careful though: The costs of these greenhouse coverings can mount up, as most plastic film and many of the cheaper sheet plastics must be replaced frequently.

SOLID FOUNDATIONS

There's not too much you'll have to think about when it comes to greenhouse foundations. Usually either the manufacturer or retailer will advise you what is best to use for your particular greenhouse and it is your responsibility to provide it. Most retail outlets will supply an appropriate foundation (at additional cost, of course) for the greenhouses they sell. The manufacturers never include foundations because it is cheaper to have them constructed on your property by a local contractor (or by you).

But don't start handing out money too quickly. Manufacturers offer foundation plans and specifications for each greenhouse unit. Be sure you ask for them when you buy. If you follow these plans, or insist that your contractor follow them, you will get proper stability at the best possible price.

Glass-to-ground greenhouses usually need only two by six redwood as foundations. In northernmost climates, the foundation should go below the frost line. Other models are designed to stand on two-foot-tall concrete or brick foundations. Whichever type of foundation your greenhouse requires, be certain it is secure, level and adequate for your weather. One thing you do not need, once your greenhouse is up and operating, is shifting and settling. This kind of weather-caused movement can crack glass or fiber glass panels, twist the framework and generally ruin your greenhouse. A few extra dollars paid for the foundation of your greenhouse will pay dividends throughout the life of the unit, especially in colder climates. When the footings are dug for your foundation, remember to allow room in one trench for whatever utilities you will need. Laying electrical cable and water pipe into a trench before the greenhouse is up will save you money later on. Be certain you have thought of everything before the foundation is permanently in place.

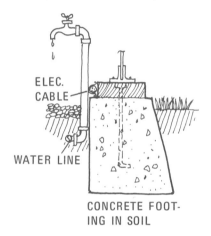

ELEC.
CABLE

WATER LINE

CONCRETE FOOTING IN SOIL

GREENHOUSE TYPES AND KINDS

There are two basic types of greenhouses: freestanding and lean-to. And there are several not-so-basic kinds including round, curved eave, gazebo and geodesic. Unless you are a true pioneer, stick to the tried and true, basic greenhouses.

Once again, think before you buy. Weigh the pros and cons of each style carefully. The freestanding units are easier to locate on your property to get the most warm sun in the winter and most cool shade in the summer. They have considerably more growing space, elbow and walking room and allow more light to come in than any units attached to a house or garage.

On the other hand, freestanding units require their own separate heating, electrical and water hookups, while lean-tos simply hook into existing utilities at far less cost. Freestanding greenhouses are much more exposed to wind and weather, while lean-tos are snuggled up to an existing building and get some warmth and protection from it. Last, and far from least, freestanding units are much more difficult to get to in poor weather. Getting there requires a coat, sometimes boots, and a strong character when the weather is really rotten, while most lean-tos allow easy access directly from the house.

The availability of extra space for shelves and hanging baskets as well as for your other plants usually proves a strong attraction for the

BACK OF GARAGE

the right greenhouse

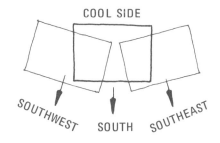

COOL SIDE

SOUTHWEST SOUTH SOUTHEAST

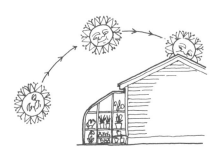

PLAN SHADE FROM
HOUSE OR TREE FOR
POST-NOON SUN

freestanding kind. However, lean-tos have another, outstanding feature to consider. Many greenhouse owners have taken to using their lean-to models as another room—enjoying them as sitting or dining rooms. Picture yourself on a Sunday morning during the winter, enjoying breakfast and the newspaper in your lush, warm and fragrant garden under glass.

Now comes the moment of truth. You have considered all the preliminary questions and made the decision: *We're buying a green-house!* So where are you going to put it? Where, on your property, will you site it so it gets enough sunlight in the winter and a bit of shading in the summer. The best location will be one in which your greenhouse faces south. If this is not possible, southeast or southwest will do almost as well.

The whole idea is to see that your greenhouse gets at least three hours of sunlight each day. Other exposures will work and you can have lots of enjoyment, but an exposure that gives you at least three hours of sunlight each day will allow you to grow the widest possible selection of flowers and vegetables.

When selecting a site, here are a few other things to consider. Scientists have determined that plant growth is greatest in the morning, so orient your greenhouse in whichever direction gives it the most morning sun.

Take a good, long look at the side of your house or garage where you plan to attach a lean-to unit. Measure carefully and mark the building with the height and length of your chosen model. If you discover you will be blocking off windows or doors or cutting across an outside chimney, you will either have to relocate the greenhouse or overcome the problem some other way. Some people love having the greenhouse cover a window, which serves as a source of additional heat for the greenhouse.

If your greenhouse comes with automatic roof vent equipment, orient your greenhouse so the sash operates on the side away from the prevailing winter wind. Any other position will allow the open vents to catch any and all cold winter winds, cause your heater to work overtime and run up fantastic energy bills.

As you select the perfect site for your greenhouse, take a few tips from people who know, Lord and Burnham, one of the leading manufacturers. They say that if you have several suitable locations you can use the following criteria to help you select the best:

• Select a site protected from winter winds by trees, a wall or a building.

• The ground should be reasonably level, to simplify foundation work.

• Summer shade from maples, oaks or other deciduous trees is good. It will minimize the amount of shading and cooling required if you plan to operate your greenhouse through the summer.

• Avoid shade from trees that do not shed their leaves in winter.

• Try not to install an attached greenhouse below a building roof where snow accumulates and might slide onto the greenhouse. Otherwise you'll have to stretch a snow guard of one quarter-inch-mesh hardware cloth over the greenhouse roof.

One other very important precaution should be taken before you dig foundations, select sites, or put the first pieces of your unit together. Many towns and counties have laws that require building permits for all structures being erected, including greenhouses. Before you make any purchases or do any actual work, check with your local building department and have them explain the regulations or send an inspector (if necessary). This way you'll be able to follow the building codes and save yourself time, money and labor.

PLACE VENT OPENINGS
SO WINDS DO NOT BLOW
INTO STRUCTURE

VERY IMPORTANT!
READ CAREFULLY

building your own greenhouse

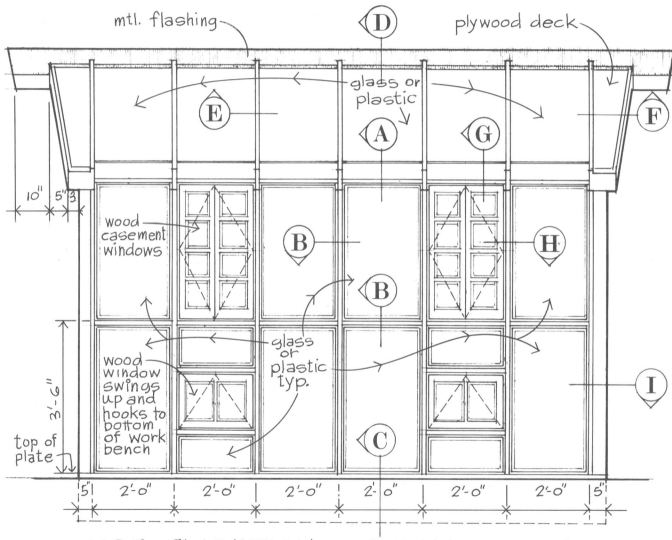

mtl. flashing

plywood deck

(D)

glass or plastic

(E) (A) (G) (F)

wood casement windows

(B) (B) (H)

glass or plastic typ.

wood window swings up and hooks to bottom of work bench

(C) (I)

top of plate

10" 5"3

3'-6"

5' 2'-0" 2'-0" 2'-0" 2'-0" 2'-0" 2'-0" 5"

SIDE ELEVATION GREENHOUSE № 1

Following are elevations and details for constructing three types of redwood greenhouses: (1) freestanding with continuous footings; (2) freestanding with precast unit footings; and (3) attached with precast unit footings. The design is intended to utilize any type of secondhand windows you may have or find in junk shops. Details are drawn at a scale of 1½ inches = 1 foot.

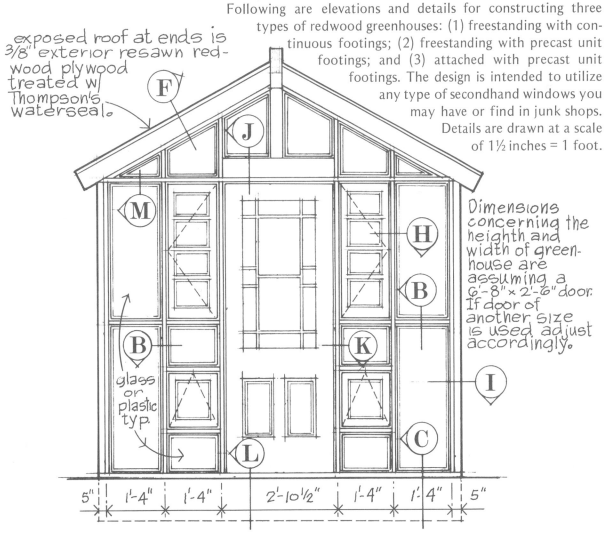

exposed roof at ends is 3/8" exterior resawn redwood plywood treated w/ Thompson's waterseal.

Dimensions concerning the heighth and width of greenhouse are assuming a 6'-8" x 2'-6" door. If door of another size is used adjust accordingly.

glass or plastic typ.

5" | 1'-4" | 1'-4" | 2'-10½" | 1'-4" | 1'-4" | 5"

FRONT ELEVATION GREENHOUSE N°1

building your own

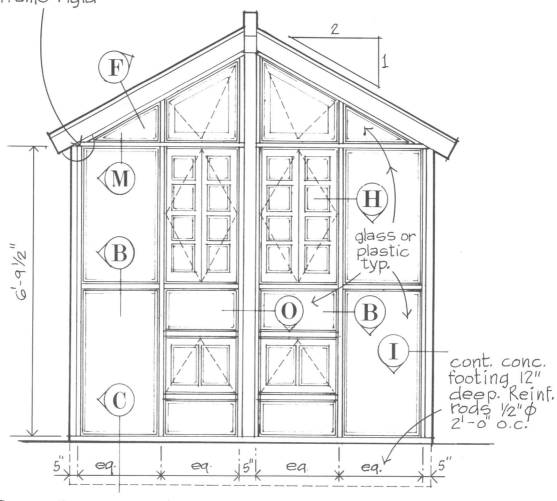

cont. 2×4 double plate all around top of walls. Ship lap and securely bolt at corners to keep frame rigid

glass or plastic typ.

cont. conc. footing 12" deep. Reinf. rods ½"⌀ 2'-0" o.c.

6'-9½"

F M B C H O B I

5" eq. eq. 5" eq. eq. 5"

2
1

REAR ELEVATION GREENHOUSE No 1

Mullion spacing between 4×4 posts is determined by the width of the old windows.

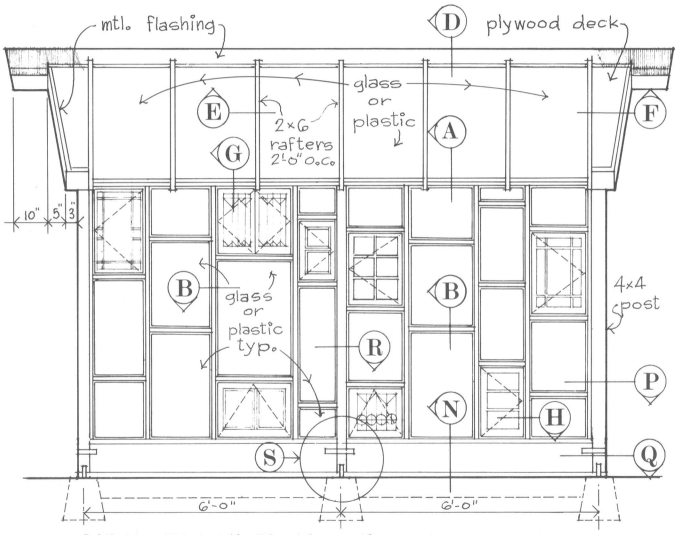

mtl. flashing

D plywood deck

E

G

glass or plastic

2×6 rafters 2'-0" o.c.

A

F

10" 5" 3"

B

glass or plastic typ.

B

R

N

4×4 post

P

H

S

Q

6'-0"   6'-0"

SIDE ELEVATION GREENHOUSE Nº 2

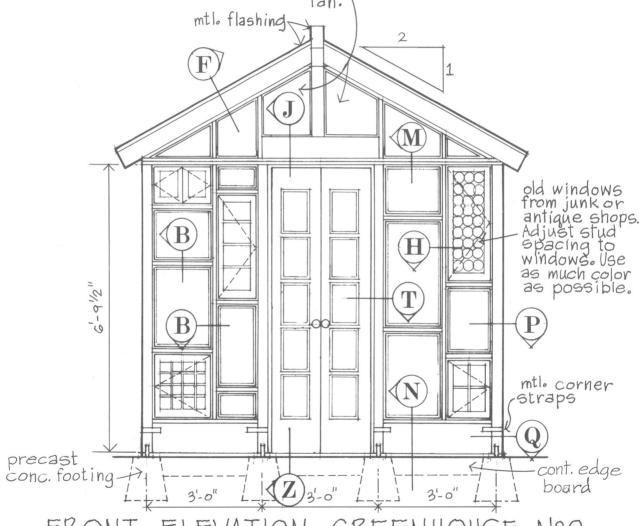

Best ventilation is along hip of roof, but difficult to waterproof unless prefabricated. If hip is not ventilated have top end panels vent or have mech. exhaust fan.

mtl. flashing

old windows from junk or antique shops. Adjust stud spacing to windows. Use as much color as possible.

6'-9½"

mtl. corner straps

precast conc. footing

cont. edge board

3'-0"   3'-0"   3'-0"

FRONT ELEVATION GREENHOUSE № 2

26

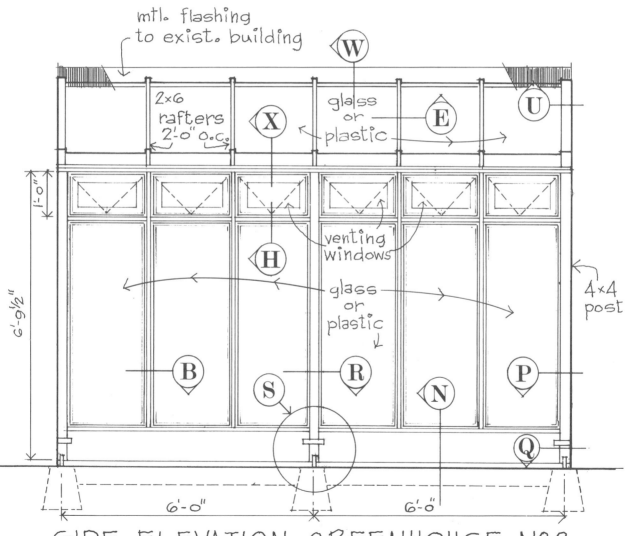

mtl. flashing to exist. building

W

2×6 rafters 2'-0" o.c.

X

glass or plastic

E

U

glass or plastic

1'-0"

H

venting windows

6'-9½"

glass or plastic

4×4 post

B

S

R

N

P

Q

6'-0"

6'-0"

SIDE ELEVATION GREENHOUSE № 3

building your own

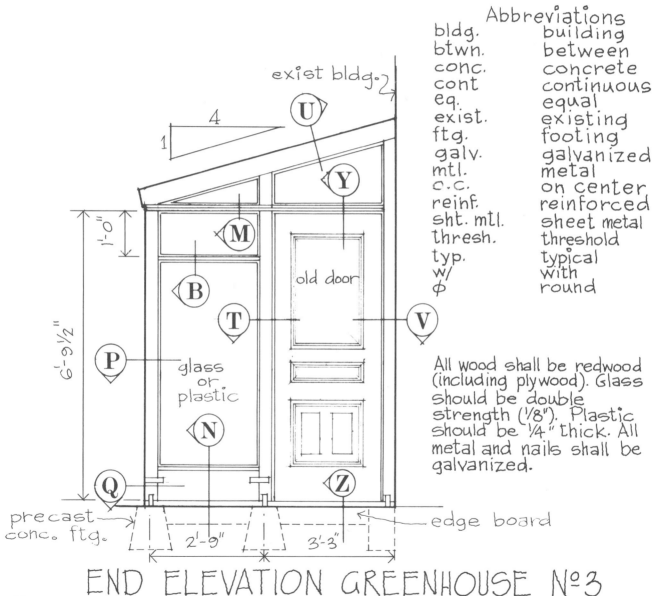

exist bldg.

old door

All wood shall be redwood (including plywood). Glass should be double strength (1/8"). Plastic should be 1/4" thick. All metal and nails shall be galvanized.

glass or plastic

1'-0"

6'-9 1/2"

precast conc. ftg.

edge board

2'-9"   3'-3"

END ELEVATION GREENHOUSE Nº3

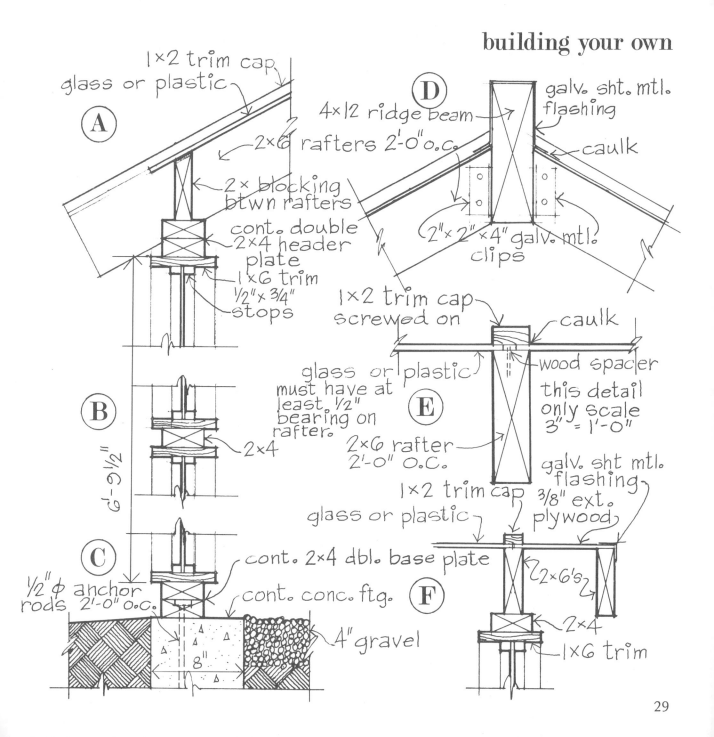

A
1×2 trim cap
glass or plastic
2×6 rafters 2'-0" o.c.
2× blocking btwn rafters
cont. double 2×4 header plate
1×6 trim
½"× ¾" stops

B
6'-9½"
2×4
glass or plastic must have at least ½" bearing on rafter.

C
½" ∅ anchor rods 2'-0" o.c.
cont. 2×4 dbl. base plate
cont. conc. ftg.
8"
4" gravel

D
4×12 ridge beam
galv. sht. mtl. flashing
caulk
2"×2"×4" galv. mtl. clips

E
1×2 trim cap screwed on
caulk
glass or plastic
wood spacer
this detail only scale 3" = 1'-0"
2×6 rafter 2'-0" O.C.

F
1×2 trim cap
glass or plastic
galv. sht mtl. flashing
3/8" ext. plywood
2×6's
2×4
1×6 trim

building your own

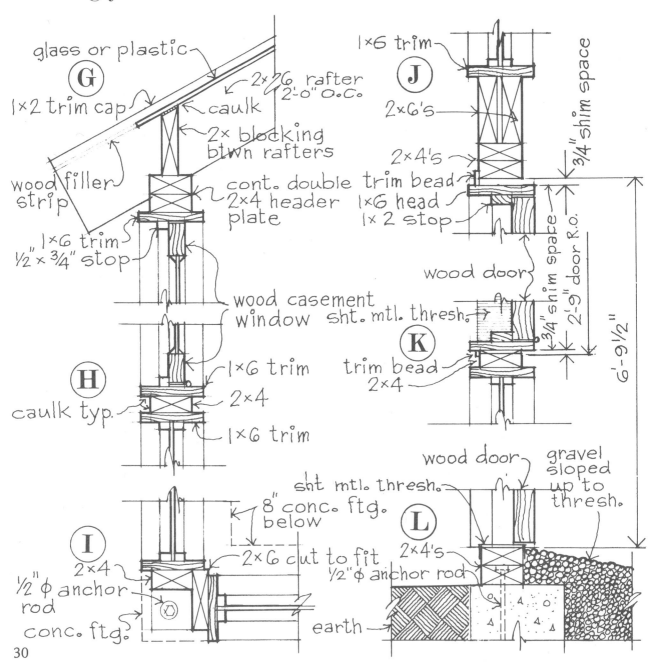

glass or plastic
(G)
1×2 trim cap
2×26 rafter 2'-0" O.C.
caulk
2× blocking btwn rafters
wood filler strip
cont. double 2×4 header plate
1×6 trim
½" × ¾" stop

wood casement window

(H)
1×6 trim
2×4
1×6 trim
caulk typ.

(I)
2×4
½" ⌀ anchor rod
conc. ftg.
8" conc. ftg. below
2×6 cut to fit

1×6 trim
(J)
2×6's
2×4's
trim bead
1×6 head
1×2 stop

wood door
sht. mtl. thresh.
(K)
trim bead
2×4

¾" shim space
¾" shim space
2'-9" door R.O.
¾" shim space
6'-9½"

wood door
gravel sloped up to thresh.
(L)
sht mtl. thresh.
2×4's
½" ⌀ anchor rod
earth

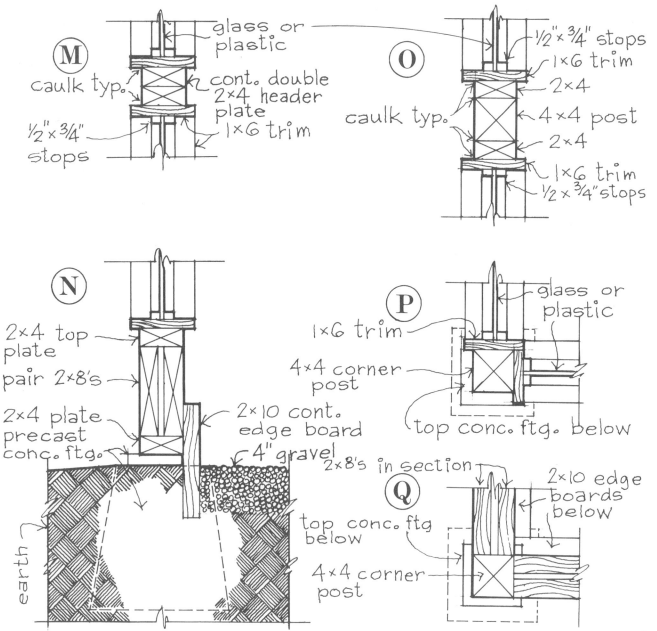

M
glass or plastic
caulk typ.
cont. double 2×4 header plate
½"×¾" stops
1×6 trim

O
½"×¾" stops
1×6 trim
2×4
4×4 post
2×4
caulk typ.
1×6 trim
½ × ¾" stops

N
2×4 top plate
pair 2×8's
2×4 plate precast conc. ftg.
2×10 cont. edge board
4" gravel
earth

P
1×6 trim
4×4 corner post
top conc. ftg. below
glass or plastic

Q
2×8's in section
top conc. ftg below
4×4 corner post
2×10 edge boards below

31

building your own

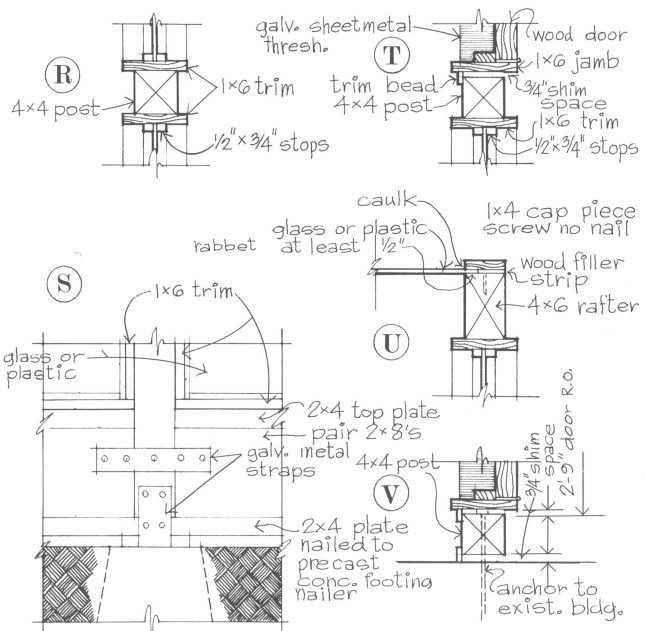

R

4×4 post

1×6 trim

½" × ¾" stops

galv. sheetmetal thresh.

T

trim bead
4×4 post

wood door

1×6 jamb

¾" shim space

1×6 trim

½" × ¾" stops

caulk

glass or plastic at least ½"

rabbet

1×4 cap piece screw no nail

wood filler strip

4×6 rafter

U

2'-9" door R.O.

S

1×6 trim

glass or plastic

2×4 top plate

pair 2×8's

galv. metal straps

4×4 post

V

¾" shim space

2×4 plate nailed to precast conc. footing nailer

anchor to exist. bldg.

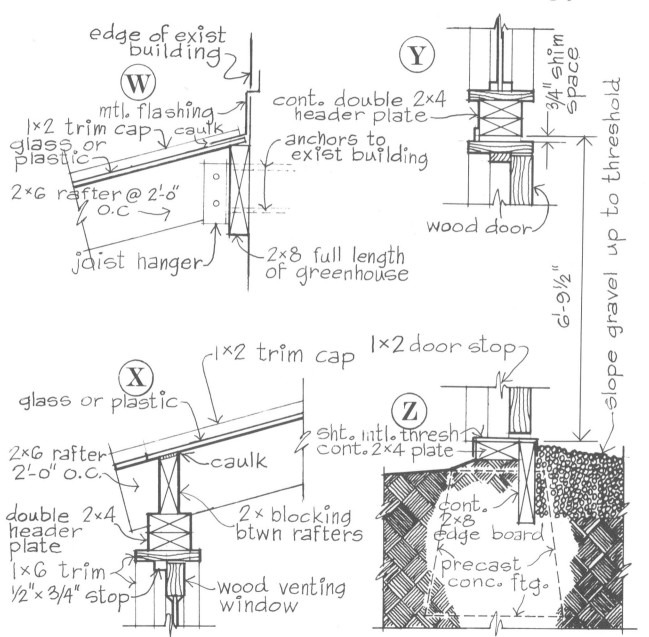

edge of exist building

(W)

mtl. flashing — caulk

1×2 trim cap

glass or plastic

2×6 rafter @ 2'-0" o.c →

joist hanger

cont. double 2×4 header plate

anchors to exist building

2×8 full length of greenhouse

(Y)

3/4" shim space

wood door

6'-9½"

slope gravel up to threshold

(X)

1×2 trim cap

glass or plastic

2×6 rafter 2'-0" o.c.

caulk

double 2×4 header plate

1×6 trim

½"×3/4" stop

2× blocking btwn rafters

wood venting window

1×2 door stop

(Z)

sht. mtl. thresh cont. 2×4 plate

cont. 2×8 edge board

precast conc. ftg.

33

furnishing your new house

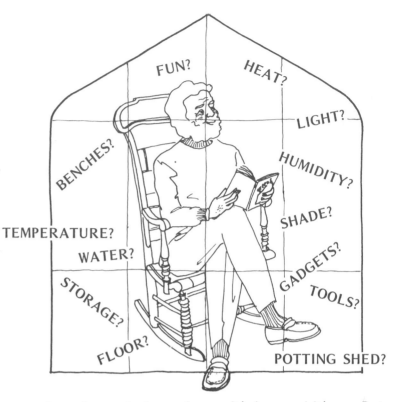

FUN? HEAT? LIGHT? HUMIDITY? BENCHES? SHADE? TEMPERATURE? GADGETS? WATER? TOOLS? STORAGE? FLOOR? POTTING SHED?

You have your long dreamed of greenhouse. It's here and it's up. But there are still a few things to do before you move in and invite friends and neighbors to the housewarming. Although your initial big investment is over, you must now provide the utilities necessary to control temperature, ventilation, water, humidity, light and shade. When you have taken care of these necessities, you'll move on to flooring materials, benches, working and potting places, as well as a whole list of time-savers, gadgets and "greenhouse toys."

HEATING

Heating, of course, is the key consideration, next to lighting (which is discussed in the following chapter). The whole idea behind greenhouse gardening is to extend the growing season from the several months allowed by nature to all 12 months of the year. Nature, of course, provides a certain amount of heat. But you should immediately ask: "How much heat should I add?" The answer is different for each of us and for you, the only one who can answer it is you. It depends on the winters in your part of the country and on the plants you want to grow, so you must first determine what you have in mind for your greenhouse. Though most plants will grow and some may even thrive when temperatures fluctuate a bit, there is no substitute for giving plants the steady temperatures they like best.

To simplify matters and help greenhousers maintain their sanity, plants are categorized according to the nighttime temperatures, or at least the range, in which they do best. For that reason most greenhouse owners choose to maintain night temperatures within specific ranges; 45° to 55°F (cool), 55° to 65°F (moderate), and over 65°F (tropical).

Almost without exception, greenhouses in every part of the country require auxiliary heat. Some areas need it considerably more than others, but all areas are subject to below 40°F temperatures at one time or another during the year. It doesn't matter where you live, far north or deep south. All it takes is one freezing night without a heater to kill or badly damage many greenhouse plants. This is one case where the old adage, "It's better to have it and not need it than to need it and not have it," applies 100 percent of the time.

Your heating unit or system must be reliable, provide the heat you need and do so at the lowest energy cost. Unlike the price for your greenhouse, the price for heating that greenhouse is not a one-time item. Your heating bill can extend for two months of the year or for eight to ten months of the year. Heat will be the greatest expense you will incur, so it makes sense to investigate heating systems carefully before you buy. You may find that such care could save money (sometimes as much as $50 per month) for years and years.

Before you do any other investigating, find a reliable source of heating equipment. As a general rule, the company that sold you the greenhouse is most qualified to recommend both the kind of unit and the size for your greenhouse. But there are times when their suggestions will not work out to your best advantage. Sometimes a dealer carries only certain units made by certain companies. In that case there would be a tendency to recommend this unit over all others, even if it is not

furnishing

PORTABLE ELECTRIC HEATER FOR SMALL UNITS, THERMO-STATICALLY CONTROLLED

GAS HEATER (MUST BE VENTED); AVOID ELECTRICAL CONNECTION WHICH MAY FAIL IN AN OUTAGE. DO NOT LO-CATE THERMOSTAT CLOSE TO HEAT SOURCE

the best unit for your situation. If your dealer carries only one brand, head for another dealer, one who carries several kinds of heating equipment, from a variety of manufacturers, and at least do some comparison shopping.

Wherever you go, heating contractor or greenhouse dealer, the following items must be considered: 1) size of greenhouse and temperature to be maintained; 2) insulation, if any, to cut down on heat loss; 3) amount of space required by heater; 4) response time of heater; 5) total heating capacity of unit in case of greenhouse expansion; 6) installation and maintenance costs; 7) and, the biggie—the cost of "your" fuel as compared to cost of other fuels.

As you can see (and you certainly didn't need this book to tell you) fuel costs are a primary consideration. As all fuel prices continue to skyrocket, some even more than others, it's vital that you pick the best fuel to do the job at the cheapest price. Select the most efficient heater you can find to do the job at the lowest possible cost. You will find also that if you pay a little more for the heater initially, you will probably pay a lot less for fuel over a period of years.

It doesn't matter whether you heat with oil, gas or electricity, or utilize hot water or hot air. What matters is cost in your part of the country for your size greenhouse. In a few years, perhaps, we can explore the possibilities offered by solar heat. Though now in the infant, experimental stage, this fantastic energy source, if harnessed correctly in your greenhouse, could be the ideal way to provide heat all year long and at the lowest cost ever dreamed possible. But at present it is not a practical consideration for a small greenhouse.

A word of caution: If you select gas heat, be certain all the fuel is burned outside the greenhouse or is at least fully vented to the outside. Gas fumes can damage and kill many plants, especially in the relatively closed environment of a greenhouse.

To get an idea of the size and capacity of the heating unit you will need for your greenhouse, the Department of Agriculture has worked out the following formula to find the rating or British thermal units (Btu) per hour.

First find the temperature difference. This is the difference in degrees Fahrenheit between the lowest outside temperature and the temperature you want to maintain inside your greenhouse. For instance, if you want to maintain a minimum inside temperature of 60°F and the coldest night temperature you expect is −10°F, your temperature difference is 70°F.

Next, find the number of square feet of exposed glass or plastic in your greenhouse. (Don't forget to add the areas of the sides and ends to the area of the roof.) Multiply the temperature difference by the number of square feet. For example, suppose you have an 8- by 10-foot greenhouse with a total of 360 square feet of exposed glass or plastic. You would multiply 360 by 70 (the temperature difference). This would give you 25,200.

Now, if your greenhouse is covered with two layers of plastic or glass, multiply the 25,200 by 0.8. If it is covered with only one layer, multiply by 1.2. This will give you the required Btu per hour capacity of your heater.

In the example, a two-layer greenhouse would be:
25,200 X 0.8 = 20,160 Btu per hour.
The one-layer greenhouse would be:
25,200 X 1.2 = 30,240 Btu per hour.

Thermostatic control is another item to be considered along with the heat. Although it is listed as a consideration, it really is a necessity in most climates. You could control the heat in your greenhouse manually, but even attempting it is ridiculous. It would require almost constant attention at all times, especially during the colder months. Automatic thermostats are the answer, the only answer, and you should select one as carefully as you select your heater. Since the atmosphere in a greenhouse is usually much more humid than that in a home, "standard" thermostats corrode quickly and lose their accuracy. Install,

TO CONVERT DEGREES OF FAHRENHEIT INTO THOSE OF CENTIGRADE:
a. Deduct 32
b. Multiply by 5
c. Divide by 9
For instance, take 70°

$$
\begin{array}{r}
70°F \\
-32 \\
\hline
38 \\
\times 5 \\
\hline
190 \\
\div 9 \\
\hline
21.°C
\end{array}
$$

INEXPENSIVE THERMOMETER TO CHECK TEMPERATURE

furnishing

instead, a thermostat that is designed and made specifically for greenhouse operation.

Another good idea for every greenhouse is an alarm system. Not a burglar alarm, but a disaster alarm. We are all fairly confident that disasters and emergencies happen to someone else and never to us. But power failures, heater breakdowns and shattered glazing, to name just a few, are always unexpected, can indeed happen to us, and, if not detected quickly enough, can frequently kill the entire plant population of your greenhouse.

Choose an alarm system that is completely independent of your "regular" source of electricity. Place the bell inside your home and have this battery-operated system set to go off if the temperature in your greenhouse falls below a certain level or goes above a certain level. In this way you can truly enjoy your greenhouse, secure that no disaster will suddenly and silently wipe out years of love, work and, of course, money.

The easiest solution to most heating problems is offered if your greenhouse is attached to your house. If your home heating system can handle the extra load and if another thermostatically controlled zone can be set up, this frequently proves to be the ideal heat source. Owners of freestanding units located near their homes should check with heating contractors before making any decisions, because frequently adaptations can be made to utilize heat from the home system.

Whichever heating system you prefer and whichever you feel is most economical, put in plenty of investigative time with several vendors so you are certain of getting the best unit—one that costs no more than you need to pay and will do the best job over the long run. The time and effort you put in researching will pay off: Of all your greenhouse needs, a heating unit might cost the most and yet save the most in the long run.

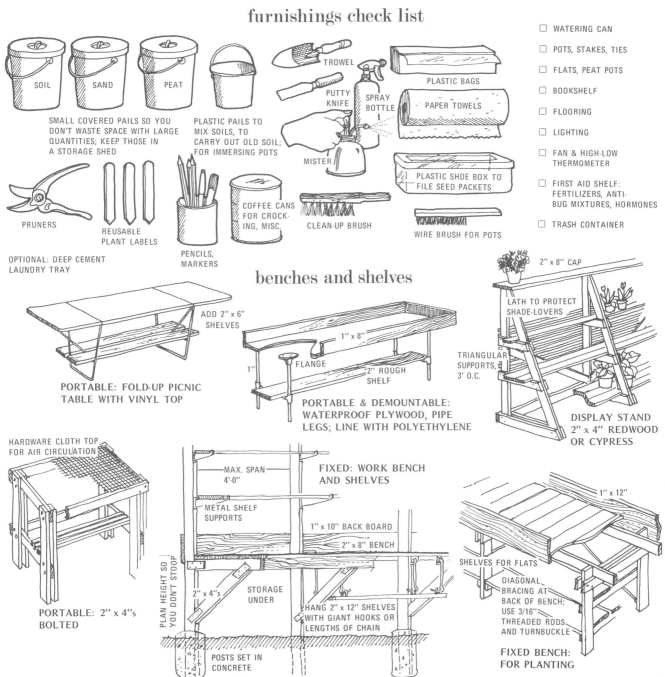

furnishings check list

☐ WATERING CAN
☐ POTS, STAKES, TIES
☐ FLATS, PEAT POTS
☐ BOOKSHELF
☐ FLOORING
☐ LIGHTING
☐ FAN & HIGH-LOW THERMOMETER
☐ FIRST AID SHELF: FERTILIZERS, ANTI-BUG MIXTURES, HORMONES
☐ TRASH CONTAINER

SOIL SAND PEAT

SMALL COVERED PAILS SO YOU DON'T WASTE SPACE WITH LARGE QUANTITIES; KEEP THOSE IN A STORAGE SHED

PLASTIC PAILS TO MIX SOILS, TO CARRY OUT OLD SOIL; FOR IMMERSING POTS

TROWEL

PUTTY KNIFE

SPRAY BOTTLE

MISTER

PLASTIC BAGS

PAPER TOWELS

PLASTIC SHOE BOX TO FILE SEED PACKETS

PRUNERS

REUSABLE PLANT LABELS

PENCILS, MARKERS

COFFEE CANS FOR CROCK-ING, MISC.

CLEAN-UP BRUSH

WIRE BRUSH FOR POTS

OPTIONAL: DEEP CEMENT LAUNDRY TRAY

benches and shelves

ADD 2" x 6" SHELVES

PORTABLE: FOLD-UP PICNIC TABLE WITH VINYL TOP

1" x 8"

FLANGE

1"

2" ROUGH SHELF

PORTABLE & DEMOUNTABLE: WATERPROOF PLYWOOD, PIPE LEGS; LINE WITH POLYETHYLENE

2" x 8" CAP

LATH TO PROTECT SHADE-LOVERS

TRIANGULAR SUPPORTS, 3' O.C.

DISPLAY STAND 2" x 4" REDWOOD OR CYPRESS

HARDWARE CLOTH TOP FOR AIR CIRCULATION

PORTABLE: 2" x 4"s BOLTED

MAX. SPAN 4'-0"

METAL SHELF SUPPORTS

PLAN HEIGHT SO YOU DON'T STOOP

2" x 4"s

STORAGE UNDER

POSTS SET IN CONCRETE

FIXED: WORK BENCH AND SHELVES

1" x 10" BACK BOARD

2" x 8" BENCH

HANG 2" x 12" SHELVES WITH GIANT HOOKS OR LENGTHS OF CHAIN

1" x 12"

SHELVES FOR FLATS

DIAGONAL BRACING AT BACK OF BENCH; USE 3/16" THREADED RODS AND TURNBUCKLE

FIXED BENCH: FOR PLANTING

furnishing

AUTOMATIC
ROOF VENT
OPENER
(HYDRAULIC)

VENTILATION

Once you have solved the "how to keep it warm" problem, you will find yourself confronted with the "how to cool it off" problem. Actually it is more accurately the "how to provide adequate ventilation" problem. You must be able to: 1) get fresh air (with its built-in carbon dioxide) into your greenhouse; 2) control the level of humidity and 3) control the heat level by venting to the outside the very hot air that rises to the top. Ventilation takes care of all three "musts."

As you will notice the first time you step into your greenhouse on a sunny day, greenhouses are heat collectors. The heat buildup in an unventilated greenhouse can go well over 100°F in a few sunny, summer minutes. Allow these high heat levels to continue for any length of time and many of your plants will quickly die.

In most cases ventilators are located at the top, along the ridge of the greenhouse roof. This makes sense because that's where all the action is: Built-up heat and humidity rise to the top to be exchanged for cooler, drier outside air. Other ventilators may be located on the side of the greenhouse, allowing additional cool air to come in, circulate and help push out and replace the stale, damp, hot air.

As is the case with greenhouse heaters, ventilators should operate automatically (or at least one of them). In most greenhouses, ridge ventilators are automatically operated while side louvers are manually operated. Except in extreme temperature situations, this sort of set up works quite well. There are many devices available to do the job, with the non-electric, hydraulic units appearing to be the most reliable, especially in "power-losing" summer thunder storms. These automatic ventilator operators have cylinders filled with heat-sensitive chemicals. When the temperature rises, the liquid expands and moves a series of rods and arms opening the vent. The opposite happens when the air surrounding the vent cools.

Be sure your ridge ventilators are installed on the protected side of your greenhouse. If yours has ventilators on both sides of the ridge, operate the ones on the unprotected side only when there is little or no wind; otherwise your plants will be damaged by drafts. (If you, like us, are tall people, you might incur battle scars to prove how often you've hit your head on the vent handle control. Pad and protect the handle using anything your imagination can dream up: old socks, new socks, rags, foam rubber taped to the tip.)

Don't ignore your door as an excellent part of your ventilating system. Left ajar a bit, or opened all the way, it can give you any additional ventilation you may need. Investigate the possibility of getting snap in-snap out screens made for the door. In very warm weather the screens can replace the door glass, providing another good addition to your ventilating system.

COOLING

Obviously it is just as important to be able to cool your greenhouse during the hot summer months as it is to heat it during the winter. There are quite a few items available which will allow you to control the temperature and keep it from reaching extreme levels.

Perhaps the simplest way to cool your greenhouse is not to allow it to become superheated. Reducing the sunlight by shading the greenhouse in any of several ways will cut down on the heat buildup. According to your specific situation and your personal likes and dislikes, you can choose from roll-up screens made of wood, aluminum or vinyl plastic. You can also decide to use "paint-on" materials like whitewash, from commercial sources or make your own.

As you make your choice, keep in mind that slats and blinds, unless automatically controlled must be raised and lowered each day. Paint-on materials are also not an ideal solution. Appearance is sacrificed for simplicity. In addition, paint-on compounds not only cut down on the amount of heat, but also light, whether the sun is shining brightly or it is cloudy. Another danger of paint-on materials is their chemical reaction: If your greenhouse is aluminum framed, stay far away from whitewash or any other compounds containing lime. They will cause the aluminum to deteriorate.

ELECTRIC CIRCULATING FAN

furnishing

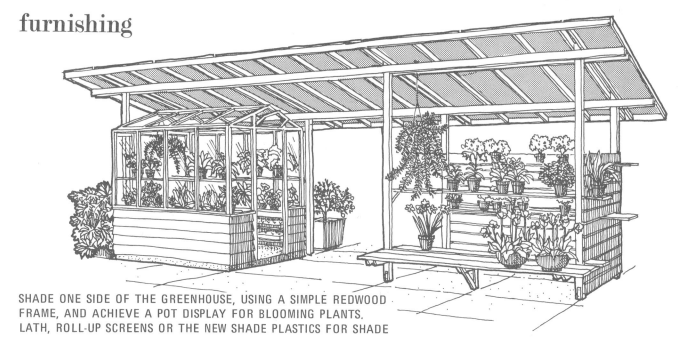

SHADE ONE SIDE OF THE GREENHOUSE, USING A SIMPLE REDWOOD
FRAME, AND ACHIEVE A POT DISPLAY FOR BLOOMING PLANTS.
LATH, ROLL-UP SCREENS OR THE NEW SHADE PLASTICS FOR SHADE

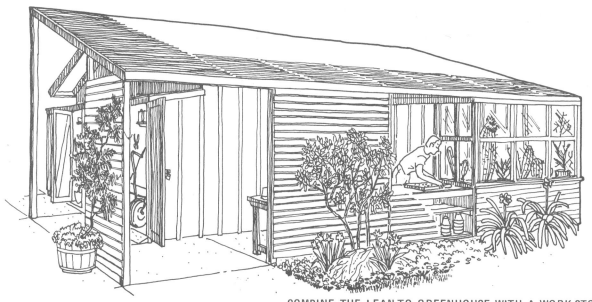

COMBINE THE LEAN-TO GREENHOUSE WITH A WORK-STORAGE AREA
ALONG THE SIDE OF GARAGE AND SHADE ALL WITH A LATH OR
SLAT ROOF: PROVIDE TOOL STORAGE UNIT AT BACK OF GARAGE

Vinyl "paste-on" shades are also available and seem to work quite well. With these, you can cut the colored vinyl to size, wet the glass area and squeegee the vinyl onto the wet glass where it "sticks" until you remove it.

Evaporative heaters, thermostatically controlled fan and louver arrangements and even air conditioners, are available to help you control temperature and humidity. Check with other greenhouse owners in your area before you buy anything. Their experience will give you the best idea of what you'll need to keep your plants healthy and your greenhouse operating at peak efficiency.

CIRCULATING FAN SIMILAR TO KITCHEN TYPE DRAWS OUT HOT AIR: INSTALL HIGH

BENCHES

All the furnishings you put into your greenhouse will reflect your taste, your intentions and your pocketbook. There is no good or bad, just what suits you. An excellent case in point is benches. The term bench in greenhouse gardening includes tables (onto which you set flats or pots) as well as units with sides and bottoms which are filled with soil and planted directly. Some gardeners don't use them at all, preferring to grow directly in ground beds. This can be quite inconvenient for low-growing crops and space wasteful because of all the area that is left free of plants. But for tall-growing plants or those with special needs, ground beds can be "just the thing."

There are so many different kinds of benches available, describing all of them, along with their virtues and vices, could fill another book. Instead, here are a few suggestions that will help you select as you go bench shopping.

When thinking about benches, use the same criteria on materials you used to select the framework for your greenhouse. Most of the problems are the same—decay, rot, maintenance and durability.

If you are going to grow only pot plants, your bench need only be two or three inches deep. To plant directly into the bench you'll need a depth of about six to eight inches. Watch the width. Be sure you can reach across the bench easily without stretching too much. Also deter-

furnishing

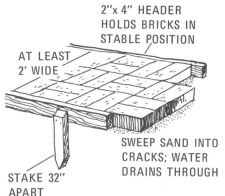

2"x 4" HEADER HOLDS BRICKS IN STABLE POSITION

AT LEAST 2' WIDE

SWEEP SAND INTO CRACKS; WATER DRAINS THROUGH

STAKE 32" APART

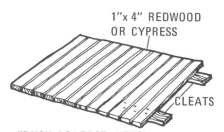

1"x 4" REDWOOD OR CYPRESS

CLEATS

"DUCK BOARDS": KEEPS FEET DRY, EASIER TO STAND ON FOR LONG PERIODS; REMOVABLE

PEA GRAVEL, CINDERS PEBBLES, CRUSHED ROCK; GOOD DRAINAGE

mine the width of the path between the benches lining the walls of the greenhouse. Too little walking or standing room can make greenhousing uncomfortable. Three feet wide is usually good for most benches.

Pick a comfortable height for you—stooping or stretching constantly will add nothing to your gardening enjoyment. A height of three feet and a width of three feet are "average," but if you are anything but (and who isn't), pick and choose, shop and check and, if necessary, custom build until you get exactly what you want.

SHELVES

Shelves, like benches, help you to create a number of environments within the same greenhouse. Plants which need a lot of heat and sun may be placed in pots on the higher shelves. Those which require shade may be placed in protected areas under the shelves and benches. The height and location of the shelves within your greenhouse will depend on the plants you intend to grow. Movable shelves are a good idea. You can then adapt the environment to new plants and changing seasons.

FLOORING

A good way to get "two for the price of one" comes when you decide your bare floor should be dressed. There are a great many materials you can use under your benches or for forming paths. Hard materials, such as patio block, brick or concrete, are very attractive and relatively easy on the feet. To permit extra drainage and keep humidity levels in the greenhouse high, the loose materials, including pea gravel, cinders, pebbles, and crushed rock, do the job best. Perhaps the best of both worlds can be achieved by putting the loose materials under the benches (where they can catch dripping water) and use the hard or solid materials for paths.

COLD FRAMES AND HOT BEDS

It is almost impossible to imagine operating a greenhouse without the help of a cold frame. Simply stated, a cold frame is a bottomless box with a removable top of plastic or glass covered with wire mesh. It is usually made of wood, but can also be made of metal or masonry. Cold frames are sunk in a sunny spot outdoors so they slope, the front of the frame being about two inches lower than the back.

Like greenhouses, cold frames use the sun as a heat source. During the day the sun warms the soil so at night the heat can be given up by the soil to keep the plants warm. In warm weather, the top (or sash) of the cold frame is lifted so the air inside does not become too hot and cook the plants inside. At night the top is lowered to maintain a warm atmosphere.

SOIL-HEATING CABLES SUPPLY SAFE GENTLE BOTTOM HEAT TO START SEEDS, CUTTINGS

Cold frames can be used during extremely cold periods, but in coldest weather they need some help. An all-year-round unit, called a hot bed, can be made by installing a coil of electric cable in your cold frame at the bottom of the bed and covering it with about six inches of soil. A thermostat connected to the cable will maintain any temperature you desire. A hot bed is actually another miniature greenhouse.

Use the cold frame to harden off seedlings and plants that come from the greenhouse on their way to outside growing locations. If you keep your seedlings and plants warm and protected in the greenhouse until they go outside, they may not be able to withstand all the temperature changes, wind shifts and other vagaries of outdoor weather. A few days in the cold frame act as a midpoint from the protected greenhouse to the completely unprotected outdoors.

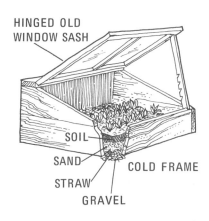

HINGED OLD WINDOW SASH

SOIL
SAND
STRAW
GRAVEL
COLD FRAME

There are many other furnishings you will want to add to your greenhouse. We have mentioned only those you'll need immediately. The others will become evident as soon as you actually start working in your greenhouse and will become more apparent as you operate it over a period of time.

soils and other stuff

Soil is soil, right? Wrong. The soil you use in your greenhouse had better not be the same as the soil you plant in outdoors, if you want to grow a wide variety of plants under glass successfully. The reason for this becomes apparent as you consider the differences in growing conditions indoors and out, and how each affects the soil.

For example, outdoors, how often do you have a rainfall that is heavy enough to be considered a downpour? In the greenhouse you have several equivalents of a downpour each week as you pour water into the soil. Consider also the fact that outdoors there is such a vast amount of soil it dries out much more slowly than just a potful does in the greenhouse. Outside there is usually more room for roots to spread and more soil (in width and depth) from which the plants can get food. A quick look at your greenhouse soil shows just the opposite. Greenhouse soil is special and must be treated as such.

Good soil—the proper soil—is important to healthy growth for most plants. We can garden hydroponically and have plants grow in water, it's true. But usually we grow in soil because it mechanically holds the plants upright, eliminating any help from man (necessary in hydro-ponics) and it also serves as an ideal storage place for food and water.

Superior greenhouse soil is made up of particles that are round and loosely packed so air and food-carrying water can get through to roots. The soil's structure also determines how easy or difficult it will be for a newly germinating seedling to push to the surface and get at the light. Let's look at the three major kinds of soil: loamy, sandy and clay. Outdoors, they exist as nature made them; indoors you produce them, maintain them and control them.

Loamy soil is made up of sandy soil and clay soil, abundantly mixed with humus (organic matter). It is nearly perfect for planting and growing everything—flowers, vegetables, trees, shrubs. When you take a handful of loamy soil it crumbles into different-sized pieces and moves evenly through your fingers. You'll be able to tell by feel that this is the kind of soil that holds the right amount of water and plant food and passes them along to your plants. For growing most plants, loamy soil is the best you can get, indoors and out.

Sandy soil is very light, doesn't hold together and allows water and plant food to drain right out. Drizzle it through your fingers and it's just a bit firmer than beach sand, running through your fingers very quickly. Many plants can be grown in this kind of soil, but to keep them growing well you must feed them very often. If you don't, the plants will suffer, for plant food moves rapidly through sandy soil, only nourishing the roots briefly. To make sandy soil into loamy soil requires the addition of organic matter, such as peat moss, humus and compost.

Clay soil can also be a problem because it is very heavy and the particles stick together. This kind of soil, when used in a bench, is difficult to break up and make ready for seed. Imagine a tiny, poor, just-germinated seedling trying to break through. Clay soil holds lots of water, but when it finally dries out, a crust forms and water cannot get through to the plants' roots. The cure for clay soil is plenty of organic matter, again, and some sand—all mixed thoroughly and deeply.

GOOD DRAINAGE:
LOAMY SOIL (SAND
& HUMUS IN CLAY)

SANDY SOIL NEEDS
PEAT MOSS, HUMUS
& COMPOST TO MAKE
IT LOAMY

POOR DRAINAGE:
CLAY SOIL NEEDS
ORGANIC MATTER
& SAND

soils

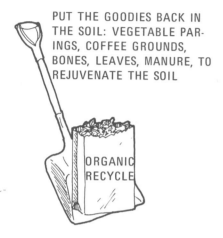

PUT THE GOODIES BACK IN THE SOIL: VEGETABLE PARINGS, COFFEE GROUNDS, BONES, LEAVES, MANURE, TO REJUVENATE THE SOIL

SOIL RECIPE

1 part LOAM
1 part SAND*
1 part ORGANIC MATTER

CACTUS RECIPE

1 part LOAM
1 part ORGANIC COMPOST
2 parts SAND*

*BUILDERS' SAND, *NOT* BEACH

Organic matter is vital to good gardening. It is also a vital part of a sound bargain with nature: If you take something out of the soil, put something back into the soil. It's a fair bargain which works equally well, indoors and outdoors. The simplest and most comprehensive definition of the many different kinds of organic matter would be "any part of anything that once lived." These include any wastes or by-products from animals and vegetables: potato skins, coffee grounds, animal bones, grass, leaves, manure, to name just a few. Many waste items we consider garbage and throw away, can and should be put back into the soil to feed it and keep it in good shape for growing new plants.

Every batch of soil should contain: some good garden loam that is rich, firm, supports the plant and holds food and water; some sand, the coarse builders' kind, to make the soil porous and also allow water to drain through; and humus, peat moss or other organic materials, to hold moisture and supply much of the plant food. Very often, the soil mixture can mean the difference between a plant that will thrive and one that will just manage to live.

Of the soils that you prepare yourself, the one described as the "basic" mixture is also referred to as 1:1:1 and consists of one part each of loam, organic material and sand. *Use this basic 1:1:1 potting mixture for all plants unless specific additions or deletions are suggested.* To give your plants an even better chance to grow exceptionally well, you can customize the soil even more. It makes sense that different plants, coming from such a wide variety of outdoor growing environments, will do better in different mixtures.

Think of cacti and succulents: plants that come from hot, dry, desertlike areas. Think of how dry and sandy their environment is. In your greenhouse, make them feel more at home by mixing one part garden soil, one part organic matter and *two* parts sand, a soil mixture created especially for them—one that is *one-half* sand. Next, think of the plants that grow under almost completely opposite growing conditions: those from the tropics with large, beautiful leaves. These foliage plants will be happy growing in a mixture that is two parts garden loam, two parts organic matter and only *one* part sand. They prefer a mixture that is only *one-fifth* sand.

If you are a white-glove gardener and would rather not do any mixing, you can buy all these special mixtures, ready-made, at garden-supply shops, nurseries, supermarkets and other outlets. All you need do is read the label on the bag. It will tell you exactly what kind of mixture you are getting. The label will also tell you that the soil has been sterilized. This means there will be no other seeds, germs or diseases growing in the soil you are bringing home for your plants—a factor of vital importance in your greenhouse.

If, however, you'd rather do-it-yourself, you can sterilize your own soil. Put the soil mixture and one cup of water for each gallon of mixture into a shallow metal pan and bake in the oven at 180° for 45 minutes. Cool the soil for at least 24 hours and then use it as you would the ready-to-use potting soil you can buy at the store.

The special seed-starting soil components, sphagnum moss, vermiculite and perlite, are discussed in Chapter 7, but they too are available "ready-to-use" at most nursery or garden stores.

TO ELIMINATE ODORS WHILE STERILIZING SOIL, PLACE IT IN A PLASTIC TURKEY-ROASTING BAG, TIE END & PIERCE PLASTIC IN TWO PLACES

ALKALINITY

To be somewhat scientific and have more fun at the same time, make a soil test. This gives you a chance to play an even greater role in the success or failure of your plants. Determining soil alkalinity is your aim. Each plant does best at a specific alkalinity level. This doesn't mean that most plants will only do well if the soil is at the exact level they prefer. It only means that some plants will do even better than ever in soil with the proper pH (the term used to indicate the acidity or alkalinity of soil).

Simply stated, soil with a pH of 4.0 is very acid, soil with a pH of 7.0 is neutral and soil with a pH of 8.0 is alkaline. To most gardeners' relief, the majority of commonly grown plants fall into the middle range of pH (6.0 to 7.0), so commercially prepared soil mixes are acceptable. If you choose, however, to grow your plants in soil of the

soils

optimum pH level, use a soil testing kit or send samples to your local cooperative extension service for analyzing. Here are some commonly grown greenhouse plants and the pH range at which they do best.

Abutilon: 5.5-6.5
African violet: 6.0-7.0
Aglaonema: 5.0-6.0
Amaryllis: 5.5-6.5
Anthurium: 5.0-6.0
Araucaria: 5.0-6.0
Aspidistra: 4.0-5.5

Begonia: 5.5-7.0
Bird of paradise: 6.0-6.5
Bird's nest fern: 5.0-5.5
Bloodleaf: 5.5-6.5

Cactus: 4.5-6.0
Caladium: 6.0-7.5
Calla-lily: 6.0-7.0
Carnation: 6.0-7.5
Christmas cactus: 5.0-6.5
Chrysanthemum: 5.5-7.5
Cineraria: 5.5-7.0
Colcus: 6.0-7.0
Columnea: 4.5-5.5
Crassula: 5.0-6.0
Crocus: 6.0-8.0
Croton: 5.0-6.0
Cyclamen: 6.0-7.0

Dieffenbachia: 5.0-6.0
Dracaena: 5.0-6.0

English ivy: 6.0-8.0
Episcia: 6.0-7.0

Ferns: 4.5-6.5
Fittonia: 5.5-6.5
Freesia: 6.0-7.5
Fuchsia: 5.5-6.5

Gardenia: 5.0-6.0
Geranium: 6.5-8.0
Gloxinia: 5.5-6.5
Grape ivy: 5.0-6.5
Gynura: 5.5-6.5

Hibiscus: 6.0-8.0
Hyacinth: 6.5-7.5
Hydrangea, blue: 4.0-5.0
Hydrangea, white: 6.0-8.0

Impatiens: 5.5-6.5
Iresine: 5.5-6.5
Ivy: 6.0-8.0

Lemon plant: 6.0-7.5
Lettuce: 6.0-7.0

Maranta: 5.0-6.0
Monstera: 5.0-6.0

Narcissus: 6.0-7.0

Onion: 6.0-6.7
Orchid: 4.5-5.5

Passion vine: 6.0-7.0
Peperomia: 5.0-6.0
Philodendron: 5.0-6.0
Poinsettia: 5.0-6.0
Pothos: 5.0-6.0

Roses: 6.0-7.0
Rubber plant: 5.0-6.0

Sansevieria: 4.5-7.0
Shrimp plant: 5.5-6.5
Snowdrop: 6.0-8.0

Tolmiea: 5.0-6.0
Tomato: 5.5-6.7
Tradescantia: 5.0-6.0
Tulip: 6.0-7.0

Zinnia: 6.0-7.5

LIME, OR POWDERED LIMESTONE, IS HORTI-CULTURAL GRADE TO BE USED ON PLANTS WHICH NEED AN ANTI-ACID

SULFUR OR ALUMINUM SULFATE MAKES SOIL MORE ACIDIC

USE BOTH ONLY AS DIRECTED ON THE PACKAGE BY MANUFACTURER

If, on testing, your soil proves to be too acidic for a certain plant, add lime to neutralize it a bit (to bring a 5.5 reading up to a 7.0). If the reverse is true and your soil proves to be too alkaline to suit specific plants, remedy the situation by adding sulfur or aluminum sulfate to make your soil more acidic.

FERTILIZER

For plants to grow well, to produce flowers, fruit or abundant foliage, they need oxygen and carbon (which they get from the air), hydrogen (from water, along with additional oxygen) and food (which they must get from the soil). Their food is in the form of nitrogen (N), phosphorus (P), potassium (K) and 13 other nutrients, all of which must come from the soil.

Nitrogen, phosphorus and potassium are major food elements needed in large quantities by plants. Nitrogen produces lush green foliage, strong stems and healthy growing plants. Phosphorus results in good root growth, flowers and seeds, in that order. Potassium is a growth stabilizer and general all-around disease resister. The other elements, trace elements, are needed only in minute quantities and are generally available in commercial fertilizers.

The easiest way to put these nutrients, plant foods or fertilizers into your soil is the same way many of us put them into ourselves—out of a box, bag or a bottle. There are at least 150 different kinds of chemical, man-made fertilizers that you can buy and use on your soil. The almost limitless combinations of chemicals allow you to select the exact mixtures, the right prescription for your soil.

How do you know how much N, P, or K is in each bag? The law requires that the percentages of each of these major elements be marked on the fertilizer container. A knowledge of your plants' requirements and the available fertilizer combinations will help you select the ideal formula. For example, a fertilizer high in nitrogen would be identified as 10-6-4, which means it contains, in addition to trace elements, a ratio of 10 pounds nitrogen to six pounds phosphorus to four pounds potassium per 100 pounds of fertilizer.

For most greenhouse plants a 20-10-10 combination works best. However, there are specific combinations for specific plants. Check the listing on the container before you buy and long before you apply. For example, we use 5-15-10 (high phosphorus for lush flowers) for our African violets and 23-19-17 for many other plants.

GIVES GREEN FOLIAGE, STURDY STEMS, HEALTH

N
NITROGEN

GIVES GOOD ROOTS, FLOWERS & SEEDS

P

PHOSPHORUS

GIVES GROWTH & DISEASE RESISTANCE

K
POTASSIUM

soils

NEW PVC COMPOST BIN CONVERTS GRASS, LEAVES, KITCHEN LEFT-OVERS INTO RICH ORGANIC FOOD

COMPOSTING

The alternative to commercial fertilizers—and many people believe it is the best way—is nature's way. This requires replacing what is taken from the soil with something that is somewhat the same. You are removing organic matter—flowers, fruits, vegetables and plants—from the soil, so it makes sense that a similar type of organic matter must go back into the soil. As we have suggested, weeds, grass clippings and other once green things, along with just about everything else that once grew, make fine additions to the soil once they have been composted.

One word of caution: Chemical fertilizers are balanced to contain the proper proportions of everything that your plants need. But organic materials are high in some requirements and lacking in others. To compensate for its unusually high nitrogen levels, plant matter must be supplemented with other organic materials. There are several ways you can add the necessary phosphorus and potassium to balance your soil. Ask your garden supply dealer for some bone meal or very finely ground phosphate rock to supply the phosphorus. Get some of the other rock dusts and powders, including that made from granite and potash, to supply the important potassium ingredient for your plants. If you have a wood-burning fireplace or know someone who does, add the ashes, just as they come from the fireplace, to the soil to provide natural potassium. Hardwood ashes are the best.

To prepare compost, select a small spot in a convenient location. If you are using one of those new, self-contained units, appearance is not a problem. If not, place the heap out of sight if possible. Use only vegetable matter because it decomposes more quickly, and cut it into small pieces for the same reason.

Make a layer of clippings, orange, apple, potato parings, coffee grounds, etc. Manure, store-bought or farm-dug (that's always fun), goes on next, followed by some wood ashes, ground limestone or other rock powders from the garden supply store. Add a layer of garden soil and then wet the whole thing down well. Repeat these layers until the heap is about four feet tall. Leave it that way for about one month;

then, using a shovel, carefully turn and water. Let it stand for a few more weeks and turn again. Repeat this procedure, and in three to four months, "instant miracle"—rich, black humus, the answer to a gardener's dreams.

The choice between organic and inorganic materials for your soil need not be absolute. Perhaps the best idea is moderation and compromise—a little of this and a little of that, taking the best of each for maximum effectiveness.

POTTING PLACES

Talk of soils and fertilizers invites the inevitable question, "Where do I keep all this stuff?" Common sense will quickly tell you that your greenhouse is not a storage dump. Its space is much too expensive for storing pots, soil components, tools and other materials. It is also a costly mistake to relinquish any of this valuable space to a potting bench.

Consider attaching a small potting shed to your greenhouse. This will give you not only a work area, but the needed storage space as well. If you attach the shed to your greenhouse, you'll have everything you need right at hand and eliminate going in and out during bad weather. If this arrangement is impossible, use part of the garage or basement for potting and storage and keep your materials efficiently stored and readily accessible.

Wherever you put your potting area, be sure to include a good-sized work table, several shelves, containers or bins for soil, humus, sand, peat moss, fertilizer, vermiculite and any other materials. Allow space, too, for fertilizers, pots, containers, insecticides, tools and measuring equipment. Leave tools in the potting shed; exposure to the high humidity of the greenhouse will mean you'll be buying replacements more often than you'd think possible. Remember also that the more "stuff" you store out of the greenhouse, the less cluttered it will be, the cleaner it will be and the easier it will be to keep it that way. You'll have more space to grow things, which is, after all, what it's all about.

operating your hobby greenhouse

For many years, researchers, gardeners, horticulturists and "just plain folks" have worked and experimented so we can grow all kinds of plants successfully in all sorts of greenhouses. All agree that success in the greenhouse comes from careful attention to two kinds of details: those concerned with supplying the proper environment for specific plants and those concerned with overall greenhouse operation.

We have already seen some of the ways to make a greenhouse environment suitable to the majority of plants most of us want to grow. There are still other areas of control, neglect of which can spell failure. If you can control these "controllable" conditions, and if you select plants that will do well under your greenhouse conditions, you are virtually assured of success.

LIGHT

Light is *the* most important factor in the life (or death) of a plant. Without light, green plants cannot manufacture food and will die. We have all spent time learning about photosynthesis and we certainly know it's true. No light, no food; no food, no plant. Some of the light is used by plants to make new leaves, some for flowers, some for roots and stems. Different kinds of plants require different kinds and amounts of light. Flowering plants usually require more light, and more direct sunlight, than those plants grown for their leaves. To make it easier for greenhouse gardeners to grow plants successfully, plants are usually divided into three groups, depending upon their need for light, which is often measured in footcandles.

Direct-sun plants need the brightest sunlight possible for several hours each day. Plants like geranium and passion flower do best in full sun for many hours each day. (To see the dramatic difference which results when plants from this group are deprived of full sun, place one geranium plant in full sun and one in shade. You'll be amazed at what happens.) If geraniums or passion flowers are not placed in full sun, the leaves are small, stems thin and spindly, and they seldom flower. They do their best if you give them enough direct sun in a southern exposure.

Partial-shade plants enjoy a few hours of direct sunlight but actually do better in light shade. They do best when placed in east or west portions of your greenhouse, where there is plenty of bright light but little direct sunlight. The African violet (a partial-shade plant) will flower when the light intensity ranges between 500 and 1,300 footcandles. The light intensity of a sunny summer day ranges between 11,000 and 13,000 footcandles. Knowing this, we get a much clearer understanding of the term "partial shade." Also in the partial-shade group are fuchsia and gloxinia.

Shade-loving plants grow best in northern exposures, since they are usually foliage plants. Many in this group will also grow well using artificial light ranging from 15 to 100 footcandles. They may be put in partial shade, occasionally, to keep them vigorous.

Remember also that the duration of light to which the plant is exposed controls the life of the plant. It will help determine such things as amount of food produced and time of bloom. It is this controllable factor which allows the forced flowering of various plants for holiday gift giving.

DIRECT SUN

PARTIAL SHADE

SHADE

KEEP POTS COOL; TOO MUCH SUN CAN OVERHEAT AND INJURE ROOTS INSIDE

operating

HOME-BUILT DOUBLE UNIT,
1" x 4"s, FOIL-LINED

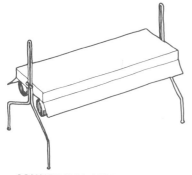

COMMERCIAL UNIT, ADJUSTABLE
CONTROLLED, FLUORESCENT
LIGHTS 24" to 48" LONG

ENDS OF TUBES ARE LESS
EFFICIENT. PLANTS AT EDGE
OF LIGHTED AREA WILL NOT
GROW AS FAST AS ONES IN
THE CENTER

ARTIFICIAL LIGHTING

In cases where, for one reason or another, there is not enough light to grow certain plants, you have two choices. You can either give up any idea of successfully growing these plants or you can use an artificial light source. There are many different kinds and types of artificial fixtures available in garden shops and hardware stores. The following suggestions can help you get the most light for the least money.

Cost, practicality and performance are much more important than fancy designs, special fixtures or custom arrangements. You can easily put together your own artificial light setup from inexpensive (wait for the frequent sales) fluorescent fixtures made for shops and work benches and available at discount, lighting and hardware stores. These fixtures come in various lengths with and without reflectors.

Keep in mind that the longer fluorescent tubes are less efficient than the shorter ones. All fluorescents have greater light intensity toward the center of the tubes with considerable falloff at the ends. To give you an idea of the cost to operate, a 40-watt fluorescent tube gives off more light than a 100-watt incandescent bulb, but uses less than one-half the energy.

There is considerable controversy surrounding the question, "Which bulbs should I buy?" There are many "special" bulbs available in addition to ordinary fluorescents and all (including the ordinary tubes), according to tests, work equally well. Check with other greenhouse gardeners before you make your selection. Then, experiment with various kinds until you find the combination that does best for you.

Start with regular, cool-white fluorescents which most closely approximate the amounts of red and blue light necessary for plant growth. The red light encourages blossoming and the blue light foliage. Mix in some daylight fluorescent lamps which have good blue but not enough red. Next try adding warm whites and natural white bulbs which have good red but not enough blue. Don't forget the special plant-growth lamps available. They too are excellent, as are the newer, high-output bulbs.

While you are buying, don't forget automatic timers. Properly set, they can be forgotten and will turn your lights on and off each day so plants will get the specific amount of light required, without any help from you.

In areas where you do not have good natural light, allow about 13 hours of artificial light each day for foliage plants and about 16 hours for flowering plants. This is a rule of thumb and is, of course, subject to your own experimentation.

Keep plants about six inches beneath the light source. That is, the topmost leaves should be six inches below the fluorescent tube. Cacti and small seedlings should be placed even closer, while low light-requirement plants, like ferns, should be placed at least 12 to 18 inches away from lights. Check your plants frequently to be certain they are the correct distance from the lights *(remember . . . they grow)*. Short crinkled leaves usually mean the plant is too close to the lights, and long, thin leaves indicate the distance is too great.

operating

TO DRIP-WATER LARGE
PLANTS, PUT TWO NAIL
HOLES IN THE BOTTOM OF
A COFFEE CAN: THIS SLOW
METHOD GIVES DEEP MOISTURE

A BOWL OF WATER AND
FLEXIBLE TUBING CAN
SYPHON WATER INTO SEVERAL
SMALL PLANTS AT ONE TIME

Plants dry out faster under artificial lights, especially during winter months, so increase the amount of water in the air directly surrounding the plants when more humidity is necessary. Set pots in trays filled with pebbles or gravel. Frequently pour water into the trays so the rocks are always moist but the plants do not sit in water. Also increase the amount of water in the air directly surrounding the plants, by spray-misting or placing barrels of water near them. Use slightly richer potting soil for plants under lights. Faster growth under lights requires a bit more food and nutrients.

WATER

Water is, of course, a very important ingredient and without it, even the hardiest plants, even cacti, will die. But equally important, you can overdo it. Too much water kills more plants than not enough water.

Water your plants when they *need* water, not according to a prearranged schedule you've established. Every Tuesday, Thursday and Saturday may be a good schedule for some chores, like taking out the garbage, but it is definitely not good for watering plants. There are too many factors that can and do affect the amount of water each plant needs day by day and week by week.

For example, in how much soil is the plant growing? Is it growing in the ground, in a bench or in a pot? If it is in the ground, it will require less frequent watering. What size pot? A smaller pot will call for more frequent applications. Is the pot plastic or clay? Plastic pots hold moisture better than clay ones, and thus need less frequent watering.

How about the temperature in your greenhouse? Is it a cool greenhouse? If so, you will have to water less often than if it has moderate heat. And, when a plant is growing well, making new leaves and flowering, it needs more water than when it is in a resting period.

If you don't water your plants on prearranged days, how do you know when they need to be watered? Look at the soil. Touch it with your fingers. Rub and crumble some of it between your fingers. Does it feel dry? If it does, it's time to water. Follow this procedure every day and never allow the soil to become completely dry. Very few plants do well in soil that is completely dried out.

Always water your plants in the morning and always use water that is as close to greenhouse temperature as possible. Plants get the most out of the combination of water and minerals when there is lots of light to turn these components into food. Therefore, the earlier in the day you feed and water, the more light the plants will be able to utilize. Also, allowing leaves to dry before nightfall eliminates some breeding places for insects and disease.

Some greenhouses have automatic sprinkling and misting systems, but these are expensive and, in northern climates, difficult to maintain. An inexpensive solution is to attach an ordinary soaker hose to the ridge of your greenhouse. But the most effective way to water is the old-fashioned way: Use a sprinkle head or spray head on a garden hose. When buying hoses, pay a little more for quality; the cheaper ones wear out and have to be replaced often.

It is far better to water a little too little than to water much too much. Few plants enjoy "wet feet" overnight and certainly not for a few days. Allowing your plants to sit with wet feet encourages root rot and that is a killer. Drainage and careful watering can avoid this problem.

Don't be afraid to experiment with plants, lights, water and everything else. Try all sorts of combinations. That's how you learn. Just watch your plants carefully and you'll be surprised and delighted to discover they'll just about call out to you what works and what doesn't.

SOME PLANT DOCTORING

A vital part of greenhousing is the ability to see when a plant is not quite itself. There are lots of suggestions on how to grow beautiful, healthy palnts in the greenhouse. Unfortunately, everything doesn't always go according to plan. Leaves turn brown or yellow, or shrivel and whole plants droop. What can you do when plants start looking sick? What do you do to keep sick plants from becoming dead plants?

operating

TOO HOT

NOT ENOUGH
LIGHT

TOO MUCH
WATER

NOT ENOUGH
FOOD, WATER

Here are some symptoms of possible greenhouse plant problems along with the suggestions of what may have caused the problem. Try to match the symptoms with the possible cause and you should be able to cure your plants.

If the tips or outer edges of a plant's leaves have turned brown, it usually means the plant has been given too much fertilizer, or the soil has been allowed to dry out. There is also the rare possibility that the plant may have been damaged by cold. Check your heater and all automatic controls.

When a plant wilts and its leaves turn yellow, it often means that the greenhouse has been kept too hot. The plant may also have gotten either too much or too little water. Try to remember how much and how often you watered the plant and you should be able to decide on the cause and the cure.

When a plant has small leaves and large spaces on the stem between the leaves, it usually means the plant did not get enough light. It may also mean that the plant has been growing in temperatures much higher than it likes.

If the plant is weak looking and has lots of light greenish-yellow leaves, you probably have not given it enough fertilizer. Sometimes, but not as often, these symptoms can also mean that the plant has gotten too much light for too long.

When a plant's leaves droop and start dropping, first from the bottom of the plant and continue on up to the top, it may mean too much watering, very poor drainage (holding too much water in the soil), or soil that is too tightly packed and packs even tighter when water is added.

If everything else seems to be OK, but you notice a plant is sprouting leaves that are quite a bit smaller than usual, think about adding a little more water and a little more fertilizer (just a little). It shouldn't take long for the plant to say thank you with healthy, large-sized leaves.

SANITATION

This has to be a key word in greenhouse operation. Allow your greenhouse to become cluttered, messy and dirty and you have virtually eliminated your chances of growing most plants successfully.

Floors and walks should be clean and swept. Glazed areas must be kept sparkling to let in as much light as possible. Weeds in pots and benches (as well as immediately outside) should be pulled and quickly relegated to the garbage can. All equipment surfaces should get regular scrubbings, as should all pots and anything else in the greenhouse.

Careful attention to a complete, carefully scheduled cleaning program will eliminate many of the disease and insect problems that plague sloppy gardeners. Check the calendar section for best times to do many of these cleaning chores and then do them as if your plants' lives depended on them. They do!

RECORD KEEPING

Unless you are the exception, there's no way you are going to remember the details of all the activities that go on in your greenhouse. What varieties of what did you plant, and when? How much water and fertilizer for each variety and when? When were certain seeds started, cuttings taken, bulbs planted? Where did you buy favorites, when, for how much and did they perform as promised? Certainly we all need answers to these questions and hate ourselves when we find ourselves shaking our heads and saying, sadly, "I just don't remember."

Some gardeners choose to use large plastic labels and write all the necessary information on them, where it is handy and available. Others use alphabetized three by five cards to keep a running record of each plant. Still others keep a daily diary of cryptic notes. Whatever method you choose for your record system, it is guaranteed to help you have more fun and more success in your greenhouse. The little extra time it takes to make a few notes will be quickly repaid—next time, and next year, with better plants more easily grown.

seed starting can be fun

Once you have a greenhouse, seed starting can be fun. One of the oldest clichés, thrown around when things are not going too well, is, "Someday we'll look back at this and laugh." Before we had our greenhouse there were a few times we didn't feel like laughing. One of those was seed starting time! Potting soil, peat pots, seeds, flats, spoons, watering cans, newspaper. Everything came together in our kitchen for that grand old game, "Let's start our seeds." The game's finale always was, "Where do we put them once they are potted?" Under tables, under desks, behind toasters . . . you name it and we had seed flats waiting there. Well, all that's behind us now and we don't regret that loss one bit. We're now very smug. We do our seed starting *in the greenhouse.*

Before you start your seeds you must decide what you want to grow, how and why. Are you going to grow flowers, vegetables or both? Are you growing them for later transplanting outdoors, into attractive containers, into your garden, or will they remain in the greenhouse? Are you growing them for fun or for food? The answers to these questions will help you determine what seeds you'll buy and ultimately, how you will plant them.

A word about seed. Just because you will now have more room for seedlings doesn't mean you should "buy one of each" that the nursery or catalog offers. Easy does it; remember there is always next year. Choose carefully. Make sure the seed is the best variety for the preferences of your family, and that it is strong enough and hardy enough for your area. If your area tends toward one problem or disease or another, make sure the variety you select is resistant to that disease.

Always buy brands you can trust. There are *no* seed bargains. When you realize how many seeds you get for your 50- or 75-cent price, you will agree it is foolish to even think about bargains. You've already got quite a bargain right there. And before you get carried away putting seeds into flats, read the back of the package: Make sure those particular seeds need to be started indoors. They may do just as well, or even better, being planted directly outdoors. Watch for the expiration date on the package, too. Old seeds will not sprout as well as fresh ones.

SEED-STARTING MEDIUMS

Next, select your growing medium. There are quite a few from which to choose, and probably as many "secret" combinations as there are gardeners. Here are some guidelines to make your own.

There is something available at all nurseries called "seed starting soil." Certainly no mystery about that one. It is an excellent medium and can be bought ready to use. No muss, no fuss, no bother.

To make your own seed-starting mixture, you can combine one part peat moss, milled sphagnum moss or leaf mold with one part vermiculite or perlite and one part loam. Add some coarse sand for plants with high drainage requirements. Some pros and cons of the materials follow.

Milled sphagnum moss is aerated, mashed, smashed and generally made light and fluffy. A terrific growing medium which permits excellent

MILLED SPHAGNUM
(DULL BROWN)

VERMICULITE (MICA)
HOLDS MOISTURE

PERLITE (WHITE ASH)
HOLDS MOISTURE

seed starting

COMPRESSED PEAT PELLETS: SOW SEED, ADD WATER & PELLETS EXPAND TO MAKE A SOIL POT, COMPLETE WITH FOOD

SALVAGED PLASTIC NURSERY CRATES

SMALL CANS

CUT DOWN MILK CARTONS, PLASTIC BOTTLES

drainage (sometimes too much, so you have to watch and water tender seedlings so they don't dry out).

Vermiculite is flaked mica (a mineral which breaks down and flakes very easily). Its best feature is that it holds moisture for a long time.

Perlite has as its base lava and is actually a volcanic ash. For this reason it doesn't absorb water well but will hold what it is given. Perlite is so light, seeds may float to the top if used alone.

As you see, all these media are very light. The purpose for starting seeds in a loose, airy, fluffy mixture is so the tiny, hairlike roots can grow and get through. Imagine their trying to fight their way through hard, compacted soil. No way.

Seed-starting mixtures should always be sterile. Don't add fertilizer; it is not necessary. See that you have clean work areas, clean tools and equipment and you're ready to begin.

CONTAINERS, FREE AND EASY

There are all sorts of containers for seed starting available in the stores or right in your home. Scrounge around a bit for the best and cheapest containers you can find. Here are some to consider.

Kits (containing pots, soil, seeds—all you need) are usually so much more expensive than the "do-it-yourself" variety it hurts. Of course, there are advantages such as uniformity and convenience (not having to mix and fuss with lots of soil and seeds), but for the most part, their cost is exorbitant.

Something to lay the seeds into: Almost anything will do. You can buy peat pots (of various sizes) which are perfect for the job. You can use egg cartons, milk cartons, empty poly coffee cups, margarine containers, plastic bottles from bleach (scrubbed and scrubbed again), water softener, liquid soap, and more.

Large flats or trays: You can buy these and pay a lot of money or a little. You can use plastic, metal (the non-rusting kind) or wood. It's up to you. You can also make or buy, as we indicated earlier, sturdy, large wooden benches and plant the seeds directly in them.

STARTING TIME

Where you live and the date of your last predicted frost will determine when your seedlings should be started. For most plants it takes a total of about eight weeks for the seed to sprout, start to grow and gain enough strength to be ready for transplanting (wherever it's going to go). If you are going to transplant outdoors, take the *last date frost is "possible" in your area, then add about a week to 10 days.* Using a calendar, count backward eight weeks and that will give you your planting date.

Some of the larger seeds benefit from soaking overnight in warm water before planting. If you choose to soak them (giving them a great head start), use plenty of water. You will be amazed how much they will absorb.

Before starting your sowing operation, gather everything together so you'll have what you need, right at hand, when you need it. Nothing is more frustrating than being ready for the plastic bags and discovering they are back in the house, or needing a pencil to make the furrows and discovering that most greenhouses don't have pencils. You will need: your own or store-bought soil mix, coarse sand, a large plastic pail or container for mixing the soil, some sort of scoop, containers, seeds, pencil or dowel, warm water, mist sprayer, labels, a waterproof marking pen, plastic bags, twistems to close the bags, newspapers if you are a sloppy worker, and a small brush for sweeping up.

If you are mixing your own soil, combine the components thoroughly in the plastic container. If planting directly into a flat or tray, spread about one-half inch of coarse sand in the bottom. Fill the flat almost to the top with the soil mixture. Water gently but thoroughly until the soil is wet, but not muddy. If there is excess water, drain it off, but wait a few minutes to make sure the soil has absorbed all it can possibly hold before draining.

With a pencil, make furrows running the length of the flat. Lay the pencil down on the planting mix, and press gently until the top of the pencil is even with the level of the mix. This should give you a furrow

seed starting

about one-quarter inch deep. Try to use the same amount of pressure all along the pencil so the furrow will be of even depth. Otherwise the seeds will sprout at different times, as they try to fight their way up through varying amounts of soil.

If you are planting more than one kind of seed in the same flat, be sure those you have selected will all germinate at approximately the same time. Place the seed in the furrows. The more evenly you space the seeds, the better the chance for survival of the tiny seedlings. The tiniest seeds need not even be covered; just press them gently into the soil. Larger seeds may be sprinkled carefully with a layer of no more than one-quarter inch of soil mixture. Very gently press with your fingertips to firm and set the soil. Using your mister filled with warm water, carefully wet down that new top layer of soil.

Mark your labels with a waterproof marking pen. Note name of seed, date planted and thinning instructions, if there is room. Place labels at end of row. By placing some labels at the front of the row and alternates at the back of the row, you will have supports for the plastic bag which is coming along.

Place the entire flat in a large plastic bag (the kind that comes from the dry cleaner). Use a twistem to close the bag at the open end (tape or a knot will seal the "hanger" end). Set the miniature greenhouse (within your greenhouse) in a warm spot, out of direct sunlight. Germination may be speeded up by placing the flat on top of a heating cable, or better yet, on top of a household heating pad set at medium.

If you choose to plant your seeds in individual containers, use the same general instructions, labeling each container independently. Place all the little containers into a "holding tray," then into the plastic bag.

Then, for a while, leave this project and turn your attention to other things. (With the plastic bag, not even watering is necessary.) Keep an eye on the seedlings, though, watching for them to germinate. When they do and most of them are about one inch tall, start to turn the pots or flats one-quarter turn daily so the young seedlings don't

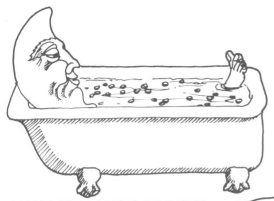

LARGER SEEDS PROPAGATE FASTER
AFTER A NIGHT'S SOAKING

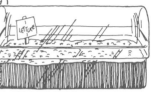

PLASTIC CAKE COVER OR
UPSIDE-DOWN PUNCH BOWL
TO MAKE MINI-GREENHOUSE

PLASTIC BREAD BOX

TYPICAL WOOD NURSERY FLAT

MIST WARM WATER
MARK ROWS WITH STAKES

PRE-MIXED SOIL
1/2" COARSE SAND

MAKE FURROWS BY PRESSING A
PENCIL ONE-FOURTH INCH INTO
DAMPENED SOIL

SMALL SEEDS NEED NO COVER, JUST PRESS INTO SOIL

SPACE LARGE SEEDS EVENLY, COVER GENTLY WITH SOIL

TURN POT OR FLAT
ONE QUARTER TURN
EACH DAY SO PLANTS
DON'T LEAN IN ONE
DIRECTION TO SUN

WHEN SEEDLINGS ARE 2" TALL, REMOVE COVERING;
WATCH FOR QUICK DRY-OUT & KEEP SOIL DAMP

THIN OUT SEEDLINGS

TIME TO TRANSPLANT WHEN
TRUE LEAVES APPEAR

MAKE A HOLE
IN THE SOIL

PLACE DIBBLE 1" AWAY FROM THE
STEM AT A 45° ANGLE; LIFT UP
SEEDLING, USING DIBBLE TO POP
IT OUT OF THE SOIL

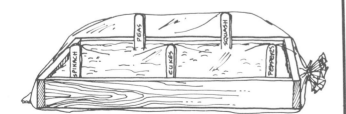

COVER WHOLE FLAT WITH A LARGE PLASTIC BAG &
CLOSE END WITH TAPE OR TWISTEM. SET IN A
WARM PLACE, WITH BOTTOM HEAT CABLES IF POS-
SIBLE, OUT OF SUNLIGHT. NO MORE WATER NEEDED

SOIL LEVEL NO HIGHER THAN FIRST SET OF LEAVES

KEEP POTS MOIST & OUT OF SUN FOR A FEW DAYS

FERTILIZE EVERY OTHER WEEK WHEN FINALLY IN SOIL

BE PATIENT: 4-5-WEEK WAIT UNTIL TRANSPLANTING

seed starting

start leaning toward the sun. Continue watching and turning until they are about two inches tall.

Now you can remove the plastic bag. Once you have done this, you must watch the seedlings even more carefully. At this point they can handle a little more sun, but the removal of the plastic bag, plus the addition of the sun, can dry out the soil much more quickly than you'd realize. Tiny roots can't cope with drying out. If you are not careful, all your work until now will be for naught, and you'll lose them. So be sure to keep them moist at all times.

TRAUMA-FREE TRANSPLANTING

You'll know when it's time to start thinning the seedlings. Although they all seem to be "your children," and it's hard to bring yourself to remove and destroy any of your "babies," you will not be helping any of them unless you remove the weaker ones and allow the remaining, stronger ones room for growth and nourishment. Be tough, be firm, stand your ground—do it. (If you find yourself weakening, stick them in another pot to share with friends.)

You may either gently pull out those tiny seedlings you have selected for removal, or you may cut or "pinch" them off at soil level. Just be careful you don't damage the nearby roots of the other, adjoining seedlings.

"True leaves" are the first sign that it's time to transplant the seedlings. Looking for the first set of true leaves is always a traumatic time for first-time gardeners. "How in the world am I supposed to know what the true leaves will look like, if I've never done this before?" is the usual exasperated question. The amazing thing is that you will. Although the expression "true leaves" may have no meaning now, it becomes crystal clear when you have watched the first tiny new leaves appear. Suddenly, when that second set appears, they are totally different, even to the inexperienced eye, and as they say in the old love song, "you'll know."

Once these true leaves appear, it is time to transplant to larger quarters. Delaying this task allows roots to develop too much and then transplanting might cut and damage them. Hold back on watering for a few days before transplanting to toughen the seedlings a bit. Water again when you are ready to transplant them.

Prepare the new beds first. If you are transplanting to another, larger, deeper flat, fill it with sand, then soil mixture as you did the first time. Using a pointed pencil, stick or dibble, prepare planting holes in the new flat (or containers). When all the holes have been completed, it is time to start the actual moving. Place the dibble slightly behind each seedling, with the point about one inch from the seedling and angling down toward the roots. An angle of about 45 degrees will work well. Push the dibble down into the soil, toward the roots. If you hold the dibble with one hand and the seedling with the other, you can pop the seedlings out of the soil into your hand with a gentle, smooth motion. Don't pull! You'll tear the roots.

Always working toward you, place the seedling into the new hole you prepared for it, allowing the soil to go no higher than the first leaves (not as far as the first true leaves). Hold the seedling with one hand while you gently press the soil firmly around it with the other. Using the mister, water enough to be sure soil is wet through and delicate roots will not be endangered by drying out. Water each flat (or several pots) as you finish with it.

In ensuing days, continue to watch and water carefully. Turn pot or flat one-quarter turn each day. Direct sunlight is not advised for now, as it might be too much for newly transplanted seedlings. Wait a few days.

When the seedlings are ready for sun, they are ready for fertilizer. Follow the directions on the fertilizer package carefully and repeat application every two weeks. It usually takes four to five weeks for the seedling to grow sufficiently in size and strength to be ready for the next (and final) transplanting.

Before the actual move out to the garden, it will be necessary to toughen the tender young seedlings enough so they can withstand the shock. This process, called "hardening off," should be started about

seed starting

two weeks before the date you had originally set for your ultimate outdoor planting date. (It is not necessary to harden off seedlings if you plan to raise the plants indoors.) Changeable temperature and sudden strong winds will surely kill off the results of all your hard work and tender loving care if your plants are not adequately prepared for their new life in that big tough world outside.

Withhold water for a few days before moving the plants outdoors. Plants should then be moved into your cold frame or other well-protected spot. For the first two or three days, the cover of the cold frame usually should be left closed all the time. Of course, should you get a sudden, unseasonable heat spell, open the top or your seedlings will cook. After the first few days, open the top daily for a few of the warmer midday hours. Take care not to forget them in late afternoon when the weather often changes suddenly and drastically. Every few days you can increase both the number of inches you lift the lid and the number of hours it's open. By the end of two weeks, the top should be open fully all day and for the last night or two as well. Be alert for an unexpected frost during that last night or two. Should the weather report warn you of one, close the cover.

You are now ready for that last big step, the transplanting of the toughened seedlings into the outdoor garden or the final indoor container. To plant them outdoors, make sure your garden soil has been prepared and is soft and workable. Using either a trowel or a bulb planter, dig a hole slightly larger than the seedling cube. Wet the soil and add a little (very little) handful of dehydrated cow manure in the bottom of the hole.

If you are planting them in containers, make sure that the bottom of the pot is "crocked" with broken pieces of clay pots or other shards. On top of this you may add a layer of pebbles and a layer of sphagnum moss to insure good drainage. Then fill the pot with thoroughly moistened soil mix to one-half inch below the rim and make a hole large enough to receive the seedling cube.

Depending upon how you have your seedlings growing, your next

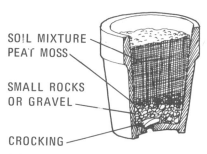

SOIL MIXTURE
PEAT MOSS

SMALL ROCKS
OR GRAVEL

CROCKING

step will be done in one of two ways. If they are growing in individual, non-organic containers, they can simply be removed from that container and planted. Just invert the container over your hand, held palm up. Let the seedling hang down between your fingers. Rap the bottom of the container sharply and the entire seedling, with root ball of soil intact, will drop into your hand. It is then ready to be placed in the pot or prepared garden hole. Set the seedling (the whole cube, soil, roots and all) into the hole. Replace the soil, tamp and firm, water a bit more and go on to the next. If your seedlings are growing in individual organic containers (peat pots or growing cubes), they can be planted as is, container and all. The container will deteriorate in the soil.

Seedlings which are growing in flats (wooden, organic or otherwise) must go one more step before transplanting. They must be "blocked." Treat the flat as though it was a sheet cake or pan of brownies. Using a very sharp, sturdy knife, firmly cut through the soil first in one direction, then in the other, just as you would brownies. You should end up with all the seedlings separated by a knife cut. Each seedling cube will have its own section of soil containing its roots. That's all; don't do anything else. Just let it stand that way for a few days. When you make the cuts try to keep them even so each plant will have as much soil and roots as possible.

"BLOCKING" INDIVIDUAL PLANTS

A final concern for tender young plants is cutworms. A band of stiff paper, placed around the seedling at ground level will take care of this pest.

And that's it. Your garden is on its way. All the preliminary work is over, your babies have become toddlers and are now starting to grow up and make their way in the world. They still need your help, so stick around, watch and help them when they need you. And, like most children after a while they will come through for you with flying colors . . . and in this case delicious vegetables and flowers as well.

STIFF PAPER
COLLAR TO
FRUSTRATE
CUTWORMS

divide 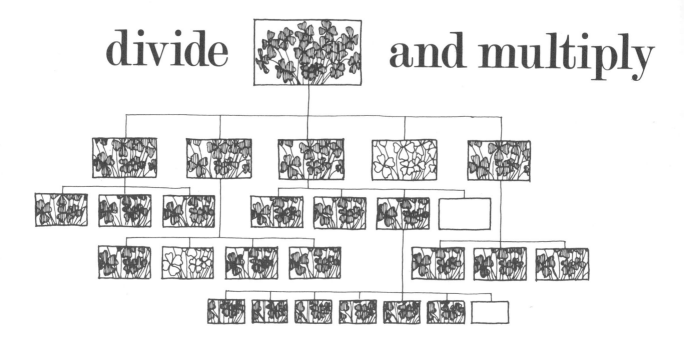 and multiply

Although dividing and multiplying are two totally different functions mathematically, in the plant world they produce the same end results. In math, when you divide you get less; with plants when you divide you get more.

Ask 10 different gardeners why they propagate plants and you will get 10 different answers. Surely you would hear one of the following: "It's a cheap way of getting more plants"; "It's a sure way of getting exactly what I want"; "I share with friends"; "I like to give plants as gifts"; or "It's fun." All of these reasons, and more, are why just about all gardeners, from the tiny-windowsill variety to the big-greenhouse variety, spend so much of their time making new plants from old.

Perhaps those arguments for propagating plants yourself most often mentioned are the cost savings and the assurance that the offspring will always be exactly like the parents. As hard as everyone who grows seed tries, as diligent as their efforts might be, they cannot guarantee, with 100 percent assurance, the new plants will be identical to the old. Plants may also be propagated by cuttings, divisions, ground layering and air layering.

CUTTINGS

Cuttings are exactly what the name implies: any piece or part of a plant which is cut off so new roots will form. This piece or cutting is placed in a rooting medium and carefully tended. In a relatively short time roots grow, and a new young plant is produced.

The two types of "wood" cuttings taken are softwood and hardwood. There is also a half-hardwood type which is half ripe, taken from the part of a shrub that is neither new nor old, but in between.

Softwood cuttings are taken early or at a midpoint in the development of a plant—the point at which the plant is young and has wood that is still soft and leaves that are just about one or two shades lighter than when mature. There is no unbreakable rule to determine when you should take cuttings. Generally, though, cuttings of those plants which lose their leaves in winter (deciduous) are taken in late spring and summer. The evergreens (broad-leaved and conifers) may be taken in summer, fall or winter.

Rooting mediums can be purchased commercially. But as with other soil mixtures, it is easy and cheaper to mix your own. Combine two parts sand (clean, sharp sand like builders use), one part peat moss and one part vermiculite, perlite or powdered styrofoam. Some plants, like ivy or wandering Jew, can be easily rooted in plain water, but then must be later transplanted to soil.

As in other greenhouse operations, have everything you will need to do this job at hand before you start. You will need containers (clay pots, poly coffee cups, flats, etc.) and your rooting medium. Also buy a root-promoting hormone powder (one such powder is called Rootone). Have paper toweling and water nearby, along with plastic bags, such as dry cleaners use. When you're all set, fill your containers with the rooting medium until they are about two-thirds full and moisten thoroughly.

Take cuttings early in the day, and work, whenever possible, in a cool, shady spot. A very hot, sunny location will quickly dry your delicate cuttings and may kill them even before you have had a chance

divide and multiply

NODE WHERE
LEAVES GROW

ALLOW 1/4"
BELOW

to root them. The best cuttings come from the terminal or tip portion of the plant. Of course, one long growth section may be used to make several cuttings. The piece you finally root should be no less than two inches (otherwise you have practically nothing to root) and not longer than six inches (or they tend to wilt).

Use a very sharp, clean razor blade or an equally sharp, clean knife. Make your cut on about a 45-degree angle to expose as much area as possible for rooting. Strip off all the leaves on the lower third of the cutting. Place the cutting between two pieces of moist paper toweling. Lay everything out so you complete your steps in order, going immediately from one to the other without a break. Have everything completely ready and waiting, as you would in the kitchen when preparing a Chinese dish.

Using a pencil, dowel or dibble, make planting channels in the rooting mixture. Make these channels on an angle, leaving enough room between them so each cutting will have room for air circulation and for light.

Dip the end of the cutting into the root-promoting hormore powder. Gently slide the cutting into the prepared channel in the rooting medium. About one-third of the cutting will be in the mixture, on an angle. With a mister filled with warm water, spray the cuttings and medium, pressing in the rooting medium to completely enclose the cutting.

The newly planted cuttings and their container should be enclosed in a plastic bag. Use your imagination to devise some sort of skeletal support to raise the bag above the pot or flat so it does not press down on the delicate cuttings. Long pencils, dowels, wire hangers may be used to make a tent type of framework. Just be sure there are no sharp points to puncture the bag. Enclose the pot or container in the plastic. Seal with a twistem and pop a small hole in the bag to allow some air exchange and prevent the growth of fungus.

Do not keep the delicate cuttings in direct sun after planting; give them light, but indirect, shaded light. Allow about six weeks for the roots to develop. Then remove one or two cuttings from the medium, gently wash off the soil and take a good look. If there is good root growth, you may repot; if not, put the cutting back into the rooting medium for another few weeks to develop better and stronger roots. Keep the cuttings in their greenhouse within your greenhouse until they have taken hold and are strong enough to survive in a less-protected environment.

Another way to root cuttings is to fill a plastic bag about one-third to half full with rooting medium. Put about three cuttings in the bag and close it with a piece of yarn or string. Pop a small hole in the plastic toward the top of the bag and hang the bag (using the string closure) out of the way in the greenhouse. This is exceptionally good for small greenhouses because it doesn't take up much bench room.

SELECTED PLANTS BEST PROPAGATED FROM SOFTWOOD CUTTINGS

Anthurium
Azalea
Begonia (tuberous)
Bird of paradise *(Strelitzia)*
Blood-leaf *(Iresine)*
Bottlebrush *(Callistemon)*
Cape jasmine *(Gardenia)*
Chenille plant *(Acalypha)*
China rose *(Hisbiscus)*
Chinese evergreen *(Aglaonema)*
Chrysanthemum
Clematis
Coleus
Crassula
Deutzia
Dogwood *(Cornus)*
Dumb cane *(Dieffenbachia)*
Eranthemum
Flowering Maple *(Abutilon)*

Forsythia
Fuchsia
Geranium *(Pelargonium)*
Heliotrope
Honeysuckle *(Lonicera)*
Hydrangea
Lantana
Lilac
Lobelia
Pachysandra
Passion flower *(Passiflora)*
Patient Lucy *(Impatiens)*
Philodendron
Poinsettia *(Euphorbia)*
Rhododendron
Shrimp plant *(Beloperone)*
Yesterday-today-and-tomorrow
  (Brunfelsia)

divide and multiply

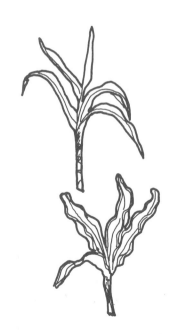

Hardwood cuttings are taken from more mature woody plants or shrubs and the current season's growth is usually used. Gather the canes soon after the plants go dormant or wait even further into the winter. Take cuttings from the base of the plant and make them eight to 12 inches long. Use a very sharp, clean knife or razor and make your cuts on a 45-degree angle.

If winter temperatures are mild, the cuttings may be planted outdoors immediately. If not, take all the cuttings from the same plant, tie them into a bundle, first dipping their bottoms into root-promoting hormone powder. Put them in a 50° to 55°F location for about 10 days to allow the cut ends to form calluses. Maintain the bundle at temperatures between 33°F and 40°F until spring.

In the spring, plant the cuttings in pots filled with light soil. At this point they are hardy enough that a plastic greenhouse within the greenhouse is not necessary. Keep the potted cuttings out of direct sunlight for about three months, and never allow the soil to dry out. As seasons change, move your cuttings so they are always in a cool part of your greenhouse. Continue to feed and water all winter. By the following spring you will have strong, sturdy plants ready to be transplanted to their permanent homes, outdoors or indoors.

SELECTED PLANTS TO BE PROPAGATED FROM HARDWOOD CUTTINGS

Arborvitae *(Thuja)*	Fig, Rubber *(Ficus)*	Magnolia
Boxwood *(Buxus)*	Firethorn *(Pyracantha)*	Oleander *(Nerium)*
Dracaena	Holly *(Ilex)*	Willow *(Salix)*
English ivy *(Hedera)*	Juniper	Yew *(Taxus)*
Euonymus		

LAYERING

Another way to get something for nothing is by layering. Layering is a method of producing an offspring from a parent plant while the offspring is still attached. The two easiest methods and the ones most often used by the home gardener are ground layering and air layering.

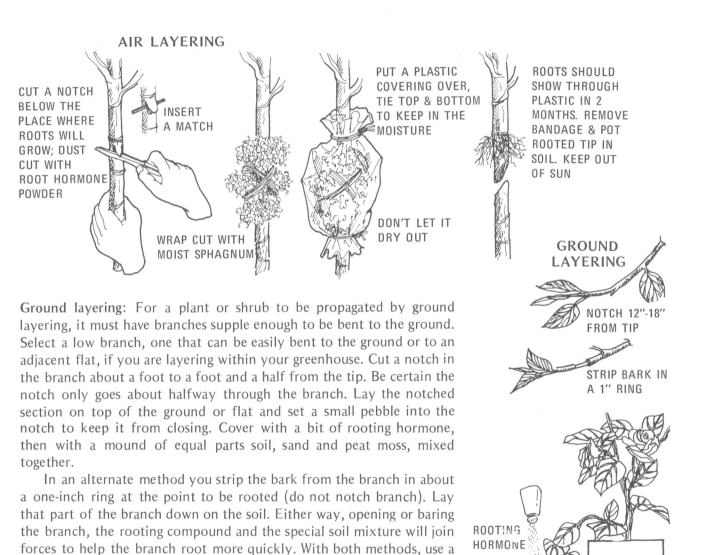

AIR LAYERING

CUT A NOTCH BELOW THE PLACE WHERE ROOTS WILL GROW; DUST CUT WITH ROOT HORMONE POWDER

INSERT A MATCH

WRAP CUT WITH MOIST SPHAGNUM

PUT A PLASTIC COVERING OVER, TIE TOP & BOTTOM TO KEEP IN THE MOISTURE

DON'T LET IT DRY OUT

ROOTS SHOULD SHOW THROUGH PLASTIC IN 2 MONTHS. REMOVE BANDAGE & POT ROOTED TIP IN SOIL. KEEP OUT OF SUN

GROUND LAYERING

NOTCH 12"-18" FROM TIP

STRIP BARK IN A 1" RING

ROOTING HORMONE

Ground layering: For a plant or shrub to be propagated by ground layering, it must have branches supple enough to be bent to the ground. Select a low branch, one that can be easily bent to the ground or to an adjacent flat, if you are layering within your greenhouse. Cut a notch in the branch about a foot to a foot and a half from the tip. Be certain the notch only goes about halfway through the branch. Lay the notched section on top of the ground or flat and set a small pebble into the notch to keep it from closing. Cover with a bit of rooting hormone, then with a mound of equal parts soil, sand and peat moss, mixed together.

In an alternate method you strip the bark from the branch in about a one-inch ring at the point to be rooted (do not notch branch). Lay that part of the branch down on the soil. Either way, opening or baring the branch, the rooting compound and the special soil mixture will join forces to help the branch root more quickly. With both methods, use a bent wire hanger or other forked device to hold the branch in place and in contact with the soil while rooting.

Ground layering may be done in early spring or in late summer. Where winters are mild and the type of plant layered roots easily,

divide and multiply

separate it from the parent by fall and transplant on its own. Where winters are severe, it might make better sense to leave it attached to the parent plant until the following spring.

Some plants that ground layer well include: azalea, beech, blackberry, forsythia, horse chestnut, juniper, loganberry, strawberry, viburnum and yew.

Air layering uses the same principle as ground layering: wounding the branch, covering it with a moist growing medium and giving it time to grow roots. This method is used with plants that have woody branches that resist bending to the ground.

Take as slim a branch as possible, only one-quarter to one-half inch thick, and using a very sharp knife, make a slit on an angle, about one inch long. Cut just deep enough to penetrate about halfway into the branch. The cut should be made about 12 to 15 inches from the tip of the branch and, once the cut is made, all leaves should be removed for about three inches to either side. An alternate method is to remove a ring of bark about one-half inch wide (do not notch the branch).

You will need a piece of plastic about six inches square—a plastic sandwich bag will do. Fold the bottom of the plastic around the branch, two to three inches below the cut, lapping one side slightly over the other so you can seal the bottom. Tape the bottom tightly closed. Then lift the plastic so it extends two to three inches above the cut and seal the sides to form a bag. Stuff the plastic with wet peat moss or sphagnum moss until the bag is about the size of a baseball. Then gather the plastic in at the top and seal it so no moisture can escape.

Your job is now finished and the plant and nature will do the rest. Check every few days to be sure the bag has not become torn or opened and the moss has not dried out. Roots usually will not appear for many weeks. Be patient. You have nothing to worry about unless rot or mildew forms, which means sure failure. After the roots appear, watch and wait until they look strong and healthy. Remove the plastic and the moss and cut through the stem just below the bottom tape line. Pot in a moist, sandy mixture and keep moist while the stem is rooting. For extra insurance, put the entire pot into a large plastic bag and tie the bag around the middle of the stem. It will keep the soil and roots in their own little greenhouse and maintain an excellent moisture level while the plant roots.

Some plants that air layer well include: dracaena, dumb cane, fiddle-leaf fig, Indian rubber tree and philodendron.

DIVISION

The easiest and fastest way of all to propagate your plants is by division. No mystery here. The plant is simply divided and the new plant potted.

Carefully remove the plant to be divided from its pot. Gently wash away the soil. Don't wash the soil down the sink. (If you have a septic tank you are asking for trouble.) Washing exposes the roots, allowing you to see exactly what you have to separate to produce new plants. A simple way to separate the roots without ripping or tearing is to place two forks back to back. Insert them into the clump of roots. Gently bring the handles back toward each other, separating the roots. Try to separate the new, vigorous growth found along the outer edges from the old roots in the center. Using only the strong, young roots, place the new plant into the prepared pot and repot the parent.

When trying to decide whether a particular favorite of yours will divide well, check to see if it has more than one shoot or "clump" coming out of the soil.

Fall flowering plants should be divided in the spring and vice versa. Bulbs should be divided when a lump appears.

Selected plants to increase by division include: African violets, aluminum plant, asters, cast-iron plant, chrysanthemum, ferns, orchids, peacock plant, primroses, snake plant, spider plant and temple bells.

When you have mastered these propagating techniques, you are ready for the ultimate—grafting, budding and breeding special varieties of plants. But that's a whole new ball game and a whole new book.

USE TWO FORKS, BACK TO BACK, TO SEPARATE ROOTS

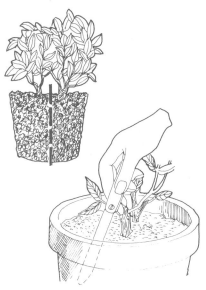

A SINGLE-STEM PLANT WILL NOT DIVIDE. IF THE PLANT TO BE DIVIDED HAS BECOME POT BOUND, USE A KNIFE TO EASE SOIL AWAY FROM POT

good eating all year long

Many greenhouse owners believe raising vegetables is what gardening under glass is all about. Can you blame them? Vegetables—fresh, crisp, succulent and delicious—that are yours for the picking. Not just in July or August, when growing conditions are perfect outdoors, but all year long no matter the cold, the snow, the rain or the lack of it. Under glass, it's always fair weather.

Carrots, beets, peppers, tomatoes, radishes, lettuce, cukes, even melons and more. Remember your first taste of a home-grown tomato? Ours spoiled us so, we have not bought a tomato in a store since that first summer; or a cucumber either for that matter. Now we know we can enjoy that same quality all year, not only with tomatoes and cucumbers, but with many other vegetables as well.

Although you may have always thought of yourself as a flower-lover, not a melon person, you owe it to yourself to try raising vegetables at least once. Many are also almost as decorative and showy as their inedible relatives. But be careful; these plants and their produce may be habit-forming.

Before you begin, decide what you are going to grow and the amount of space you want to make available for the growing. Start with those vegetables you love and would love to eat fresh all year long. Space in a greenhouse is precious; don't waste it on vegetables you could happily do without. Be miserly with the space you allocate. Onions, lettuce, radishes, beets and herbs take up relatively little space in return for a good yield. Cucumbers, melons and eggplant are space-grabbers and, in comparison, yield relatively little. Tomatoes and peppers are a must (where does it say a writer has to be without prejudice?) and you "must" grow them no matter how much space they take. Some vegetables take deep soil; keep the bench structure sturdy enough to take weight of soil and water. You may want to use a lightweight soil amendment like perlite or vermiculite, but because they have no nutrients, you will have to add bone meal. Vegetables need some plant food when seeds sprout and again when plants are established. Leaf-types take high-nitrogen food.

You'll want to grow your vegetables from seed, too. Even tomatoes. It saves money, you can start them at odd times when seedlings aren't yet available in the nurseries, and it's part of the fun. You'll find also that you will have plenty of seedlings to give away to friends to plant in their outdoor gardens. A nice gift idea.

Many vegetables, like tomatoes, peppers, eggplant and melon, must be pollinated if they are to bear fruit. Outdoors the bees do the job. Indoors, hopefully, there will be no bees, so you must do the job yourself.

When the flowers are open their widest, swish a brand new sable or camel's hair brush around the inside of the flower until the bristles are coated with the fine, yellow-orange powdery pollen. Then, without touching the brush tip or the pollen, gently move the brush to the next flower and move it around its inside. Continue this process until you have hand-pollinated all the flowers. Then stand back and watch the miracle as the fruit begins to form.

Let's start off with the efficiency models, the "small space" vege-

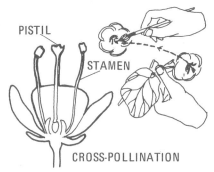

PISTIL

STAMEN

CROSS-POLLINATION

good eating

SOW STUBBY-TYPE CARROTS
TO USE LESS SOIL DEPTH

tables, move on to the space-grabbers and then look at some others you should try just because they deserve trying.

CARROTS

Believe it or not, greenhouse carrots are even better than the ones you've been growing in the garden. Controlled conditions and constant care (especially smooth, rock-free soil) make them shaplier, tastier and more tender.

Select the varieties that grow short and stubby (no more than about five inches long at maturity) or, if you must choose a longer variety, harvest them when they are half- to three-quarters mature. The reason is obvious. Unless you have an unusually deep bench, you will not have room for fully mature, longer carrots. Some good, short varieties are Goldinhart, Chantenay and Early Nantes. Don't forget the mini-carrots —Short 'n Sweet, Little Finger and Tiny Sweet—that do extremely well in pots or benches in the greenhouse.

Sow seed in slightly sandier-than-usual soil, one-half inch apart and one-quarter inch deep in rows about six inches apart and cover with a quarter-inch of soil. When sturdy seedlings are up, thin so they stand approximately two inches apart. Water the seedlings thoroughly and never allow them to dry out; a plastic sheet covering the seedlings will trap heat and moisture in. Remove when seeds sprout. Keep an eye on temperature and ventilation in the greenhouse. Carrots prefer cool night temperatures, so keep them at about 50° to 55°F or they develop a very strong flavor. Start new sowings every three weeks to keep tender carrots in continuous supply.

BEETS

Here's an easy-to-grow, colorful vegetable that gives you two for the price and space of one. The tops, or beet greens, can be cooked and eaten as a tasty vegetable, while the other part of the team, the versatile globes or roots, are fantastic eating hot or cold and also are a primary part of many soups and relishes.

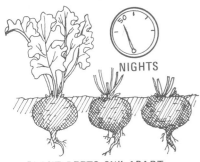

PLANT BEETS 2½" APART

Sow seed about one-half inch apart and one-quarter inch deep in rows about six inches apart. Thin seedlings to stand about two and a half inches apart. Don't throw away the "thinnings." Use them for "greens" in salads, etc. Excellent varieties for greenhouse culture include Detroit Dark Red (short top) and Early Wonder. The old-fashioned Lutz Green Leaf takes longer but is even sweeter and worth waiting for. This vegetable likes it cool and comfortable, so keep temperatures at about 50°F at night. Water seedlings thoroughly and never allow them to dry out. Harvest your beets as soon as the roots are a respectable size. The tiniest beets are the tenderest. If you get all leaves and no bottoms, you didn't thin the seedlings enough or the soil lacks boron.

ONIONS

There are a wealth of onion varieties from which to choose—scallions, white, red, Spanish or old-fashioned hamburger covers. Want to start them from seed, sets or plants? These wonderful, all-time favorite heartburners are available any way you like them.

To start from seed, sow about one-half inch deep and one-half inch apart in rows six inches apart. When seedlings are six inches high, thin them and use thinnings as green onions. Continue to thin and eat until plants are about three to four inches apart.

To start from sets, put each of the little onion bulbs about one inch deep and about three to four inches apart. When tops get long, clip and use them in cooking as you would scallion tops. If left unclipped, onion tops will be strong and the bulbs small. Clipping forces the onion to put all its energy into bulb making.

When you feel it's onion-picking time, find out the easy way. Dig one up carefully, trying not to damage any of the roots on the bottom. If the onion is not as large as you want it, put it back into the soil.

Keep your onions watered thoroughly. If allowed to become dry they also become strong and develop a bite. They grow best when night temperatures are in the 60°F range.

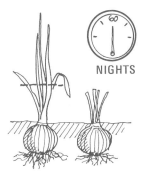

NIGHTS

PLANT ONIONS 3"-4" APART; BARBER TOPS TO GIVE BULB LARGER SHARE OF ENERGY & MILDER FLAVOR

83

good eating

THIN RADISHES 9 TO EACH 12"

SOW BIBB LETTUCE 8" APART

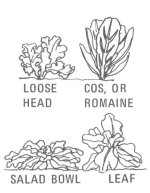

LOOSE HEAD   COS, OR ROMAINE

SALAD BOWL   LEAF

RADISHES

These seem made-to-order for greenhouse production. They grow and mature quickly, take up little room and taste even better than their garden-grown cousins. In less than a month you can have beautiful, sweet radishes for salads and relish trays at any time of the year.

Sow seeds of almost any variety (and there are many from which you can choose) about one-half inch apart and one-quarter inch deep into slightly sandier-than-usual soil in rows four inches apart. Water thoroughly and keep well watered. If the soil gets dry, radishes get "hot," so cool them regularly. Thin so there are no more than nine radishes to each foot of row. Thinning any less will produce radishes with lots of green top and very little bottom. Grow at nighttime temperatures that do not exceed 50° to 55°F. Sow seeds every three weeks and you'll have radishes, ready and waiting at all times. Try Cherry Belle, Scarlet Globe and French Breakfast for starters.

LETTUCE

If you try no other vegetables in your greenhouse, grow lettuce. And if you grow no other lettuce, you must try Bibb. There is no way to describe the taste sensation of a salad made with crisp, crunchy lettuce fresh from the greenhouse during the darkest days of winter.

Sow lettuce seed in rows of slightly acid soil, about eight inches apart, covering with a thin layer of peat moss. Once seedlings are established, thin to eight inches apart. Water thoroughly and be certain the plants are not allowed to dry out. To prevent rot and disease, water early in the day so leaves get a chance to dry before nightfall; always remove dead or dried leaves to foil fungus problems. Nighttime temperatures around 50°F and daytime temperatures no higher than about 70°F produce the best lettuce. Hot weather causes tip-burn and high night temperatures make lettuce bitter. Try some of the different types—head, loose head, leaf and Cos or Romaine—to have fun and satisfy your curiosity. To satisfy your salad bowl put in plenty of Bibb and Buttercrunch. And start a new patch every two or three weeks.

TOMATOES

If you grow no other vegetables in your greenhouse, grow tomatoes. We know we just said the same thing about lettuce, but if it's true about lettuce, it is doubly true about tomatoes. Somewhere in the middle of the small-space vegetables and the space-grabbers, tomatoes can be trained so they take up minimum space with a maximum yield.

Start tomatoes as you would for outdoors, in peat pots or other individual containers; germinating seeds need bottom heat and uniform heat to sprout successfully. When the seedlings are large enough, carefully transplant to pots or directly into the ground in the greenhouse. Be sure they never completely dry out. Once they've got two leaves, put in pots, being careful not to break roots. Because of the space limitations, do not allow your tomatoes to stoop, swoop or otherwise spread themselves out as they grow in the sun. Trim all but a single main stem and carefully train this stem to a stake or wire support. (If you enjoy Rube Goldberg inventions, work out some sort of horizontal and vertical wire arrangement that operates by pulleys and springs, giving more and more support as the tomatoes grow larger and heavier.) Remove all suckers that appear at each point where a leaf meets the stem. Suckers drain off strength and vigor.

Tomatoes are truly a warm-weather crop. They must be grown in a night temperature of about 60° to 65°F and a daytime temperature of around 75° to 80°F. However, all your work and effort will be wasted if you allow temperatures to go much higher. Tomatoes will not set fruit at higher temperatures and all you'll have are lots and lots of leaves.

Watering, too, is very important. Too much watering can cause root rot and other diseases or problems. Too little water will stunt the growth of the plant and cause the flowers to drop off before there is any chance of pollination. And, as you know, no flowers, no fruit. You must play Mother Nature if you want tomatoes. Pollinate, as directed earlier in this chapter, when the flowers are open widest.

Some superb varieties of tomatoes to try in your greenhouse include Big Early, Burpee Hybrid, Manapal, Pixie and Patio.

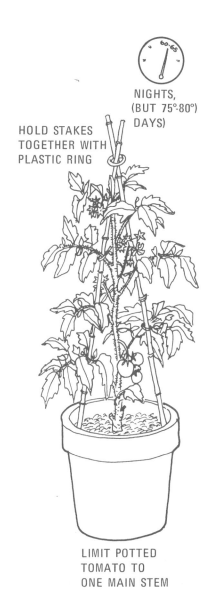

NIGHTS, (BUT 75°-80° DAYS)

HOLD STAKES TOGETHER WITH PLASTIC RING

LIMIT POTTED TOMATO TO ONE MAIN STEM

good eating

USE HEAT TO START PEPPERS;
A WATERPROOF HEAT PAD SET
AT LOW. LIFT BOX FOR AIR SPACE

PRUNE BACK EGGPLANT
TO SAVE SPACE

PEPPERS

These plants are so pretty they belong in your house as well as in your greenhouse. They are quite similar in culture to tomatoes, though much more compact growers. Peppers like plenty of water but don't like being left to sit in it for any length of time.

Use a waterproof heating pad or cable to start pepper seeds or they will take forever to germinate. Without the steady heat from the cable, there is also the chance that the seed will sit so long it may eventually rot. When seedlings are about three inches tall and show healthy, true leaves, transplant to pots, boxes or your bench. Most peppers do not need your help in the pollination process, but a little swish with your magic sable brush will assure you of even more fruit.

Everybody eats *green* peppers all the time, treating them as though they were fully ripe, mature fruit, which they are not. When they are fully ripe, peppers are red. Have a little extra patience, let them mature and turn red. They are gorgeous to see and a completely different taste experience. The best varieties to grow in your greenhouse include California Wonder, Merrimack Wonder and Sunny Brook.

EGGPLANTS

These will do exceptionally well in the warm segment of the greenhouse if you can afford the space they require. Almost identical in culture to tomatoes and peppers, eggplants can be spaced no closer than one foot apart and must be trained, by judicious pruning, to grow as compactly as possible.

Start seeds over a waterproof heating pad or cable, transplant carefully into a humus-rich soil and harvest shiny, firm, glossy, dark-colored fruits while they are small, young and tender. Eggplants are ripe and edible as soon as the fruit appears and starts growing. All they do is get bigger, not riper. There are many delicious eggplant dishes which make growing this vegetable worthwhile. For best results, start with Black Beauty or Early Beauty Hybrid.

CUCUMBERS

Try them and you'll like them; but train them or they'll try you and your patience. Train them up a trellis or plastic netting. Take a tip from the commercial greenhouse people and allow only a single stem to make it to the top of the support.

The best bet is to start cukes in peat pots, one-half inch deep, and after the seedlings are sturdy put them into a large tub filled with organically enriched soil, allowing 10 square inches per plant. Lots and lots of humus, compost or well-rotted manure results in an abundance of fine, sweet fruit. Water thoroughly and deeply with warm water, but only early in the day so the plants don't stand in water. Fertilize every other week with liquid fertilizer added to the water. When flowers appear and are fully open, hand-pollinate with a clean brush as described earlier in this chapter.

As cukes develop, pick early and frequently to keep vines producing—and for the freshest, coolest, most delectable cucumbers you've ever eaten. Don't peel them because the magnesium deposit under the skin counteracts the bitterness and burpiness.

MELONS

Try these, too, if you think you can work out the engineering feat required to train the vines up a trellis which will not only keep the vine contained but support the heavy melons as well. One way that works (and is fun to do because it sounds a little ridiculous) is to set up individually supported mesh bags to hold the melons as they grow and mature. Your own situation and ingenuity will dictate other solutions. Once you've found a way, you will not only have had fun while fumbling, but will end up with a taste worth having struggled after. Melon culture is the same as that described for cucumbers except that sprouting seeds need 80 degrees day and night. For repotting allow each plant one square foot of soil loaded with plenty of well-rotted manure or compost. Keep plants well centered. Start out with muskmelons and move in all directions from there.

CRIMP WIRE ENDS WITH PLIERS

TRAIN CUKES & MELONS ON A WIRE MESH CYLINDER TO SAVE SPACE

good eating

There are, of course, many other vegetables you can grow in your greenhouse. Experiment and determine those that appeal to you, those you can keep cool enough (warmth is never the problem) and those you feel are worth your time and effort. In addition, try the following two "specials." Your first harvest will fully justify the name specials.

MUSHROOMS

If there is any miser in you, space miser, or other, and you believe in the adage, "Waste not, want not," mushrooms are made to order for your greenhouse. They will grow beautifully in the space that is worthless for anything else. Grow mushrooms in the dark, cool, unpleasant spot under your benches. The trays take only a few inches of vertical space and produce a multitude of those delectable fungi that have been considered delicacies since before the days of the Old Testament.

Mushrooms are unusual in that they never flower and have no leaves. Though fussy, they are simple to grow if certain rules are followed. Mushrooms like air but won't grow if there is a draft. They like moisture but only a little bit at a time. They like darkness because they have no need for chlorophyll to turn green. And, finally, they do well only in certain temperatures—a little higher or lower usually finishes them.

An easy way to start is to buy a mushroom tray from a local garden shop or nursery; the mushrooms are already planted in the growing medium. Water it thoroughly and carefully with a sprayer so there is no splashing to knock the growing materials out of place. After you've tried this once you may elect, in the future, to buy only pure culture spawn and plant them yourself in a tray of rotted horse manure or compost. Mushrooms require no soil.

When the surface of the growing medium is moist, but not soggy, place the tray under a bench where it will be in a fairly steady temperature somewhere between 50° to 65°F. Water as often as necessary to keep the trays from ever drying out.

KEEP MUSHROOMS DAMP & DARK.
NEVER LET TRAYS DRY OUT

After about three weeks of daily misting, the mushrooms, looking like tiny, white pinheads, will appear in the tray. You'll be heading for the homestretch now, and all you need do is watch and wait for them to grow to full size. Pick as they become mature, when the part of the cap next to the stem breaks open. With little care and patient picking, you will be able to have fresh, fantastic mushrooms for weeks and weeks and weeks.

ASPARAGUS

Start these delicacies from roots available at most garden shops. Place about a foot apart, spread the roots, cover them along with the crown with no more than two inches of loose, humusy soil and keep moist. Because asparagus roots must stay in place year after year, plant in space you can spare. Actually, asparagus produce more and taste better the second year than the first; the plants will benefit if you forego that first harvest.

Cut second-year stalks once they reach good size. Don't allow them to get too thick; they taste like bamboo if you do. Each year for quite some time you will be able to cut stalks over increasingly longer periods. Feed plants a balanced plant food in spring. So enjoy!

HERBS

There's no way your greenhouse can be complete without some herbs. They have been important parts of civilization since earliest recorded time and come to us in song and story as well. We know of many herbs that grew in Egypt and Mesopotamia 5,000 years ago. We also know that Hippocrates, the Greek physician, prescribed herbal remedies in 460 B.C., with a respectable record of success.

The culinary herbs are a delight to grow and use. They require little care and certainly no pampering, do well in the sun, thrive in loose, humus-filled soil, withstand concentrated heat, enjoy a reasonable dry spell and, as a group, can resist disease and most insects.

There are at least 50 herbs used in cooking today, many of which

good eating

BASIL

BORAGE

CHIVES

are used almost exclusively by gourmets and culinary artists. But that's not the way it has to be. Herbs in cooking are for everyone, and with the addition of a pinch of the right herb, an ordinary dish becomes something special. Here is a sampling of the best known, easiest to use, everyday-type herbs you should grow in your greenhouse and use in your kitchen.

BASIL

Especially good in any recipe that calls for tomatoes and a natural with all sorts of Italian and other Mediterranean dishes. Sow sweet basil (it's an annual) about one-half inch deep in enriched soil. After sprouts appear, space about 10 inches apart. Keep in a sunny part of the greenhouse, feed once a month and water well. Usability comes early with basil; start clipping and using leaves as soon as plant is six inches tall. You'll not only have wonderful leaves to use in cooking but, by clipping, will induce the plant to grow bushier and fuller.

BORAGE

Use to flavor punches and other cold drinks, for salads or as cooked greens, or in pickling. Press seeds firmly into soil about 12 inches apart. Grows equally well directly in benches or in individual pots one to three feet tall in sun or filtered shade with moderate watering. Gray-green leaves may be picked fresh at any time and used, or they can be dried and stored.

CHIVES

Use to give a mild onion flavor to soups, salads, egg or cheese dishes. Propagate by division, then plant the small clumps with roots about six inches apart. Continuously snip off the tips to insure continued production of new growth. Keep in the sunniest part of the greenhouse in humus-rich soil and give plenty of water.

DILL

Use chopped leaves and seeds for fish, sauces, salads, egg dishes and boiled potatoes. A healthy pinch of dill will also completely change the flavor of a pot roast. Space plants about four inches apart in pots or directly into bench. Dill does not transplant well; it has a tap root which wants well-drained soil. Pick leaves when flowers open; harvest flat brown seeds when ripe. Dill is an annual which may grow to four feet tall.

FENNEL

Use to flavor sauces or fish and to brew an unusual tea. Plant seeds or seedlings in a sunny spot about eight inches apart in a bench or put them one to a pot. Pick stems just before flowers bloom. If you blanch the stalks by wrapping them in heavy paper, the tender stalks may be eaten like celery. Seed, picked when ripe and brown, may be used sparingly as a condiment. Keep in mind when you plant that fennel can get to be five feet tall—don't let it push you out of your greenhouse.

MARJORAM

This is one of the most popular herbs. Transplant seedlings so they are about four inches apart in soil with good drainage. They'll grow to two-foot shrubs by August. Use fresh at any time. Cut leafy stems at flowering time for drying.

MINT

Use in cold drinks, teas and to make mint sauces. Mint goes a little crazy and will spread and "take over" if it is not watched. There are many varieties of mint; select the one you like best. Plant divided clumps at least 12 inches apart in a shady part of the greenhouse and keep soil moist; mint loves water. Harvest fresh young leaves any time. This prolific herb is great to share with friends (that's how we got our first clump).

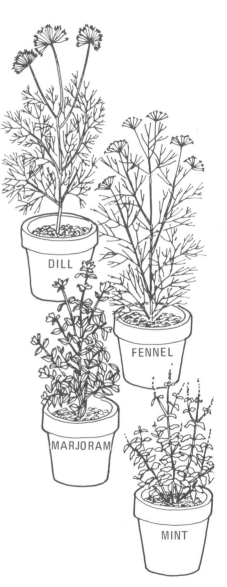

good eating

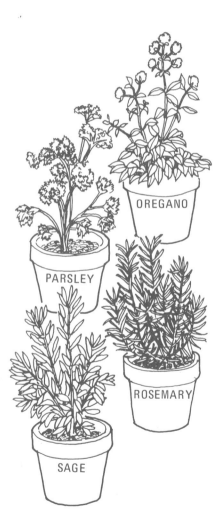

OREGANO

Another favorite for Italian cooking, this herb is also called pot marjoram or wild marjoram. Use leaves fresh or dried and use plenty to get that sensational, unforgettable taste we all know from well-seasoned pizza. These hardy little plants like lots of sun and water, sandy soil and a dash of extra humus in the pot. A rapid, all-over-the-place grower, oregano should be clipped frequently to prevent its getting out of hand. Use the clippings on fish, soups, vegetables and all sorts of stews for a taste you won't soon forget. Dry some so you may enjoy the flavor all year long.

PARSLEY

A favorite in and on almost everything, it is also very good for you because it contains large amounts of vitamin A. Plant parsley seeds about one-quarter inch deep after first soaking in hot water for 24 hours. Pull and use seedlings as they grow until spacing is about 10 inches apart. Keep in a sunny part of your greenhouse, feed once each month, and water just before the soil becomes dry. Snip and use the green, green leaves at any time.

ROSEMARY

Great for flavoring most meats. Plant cuttings in individual pots or at least eight inches apart in benches. Train on netting to keep under control. Cut fresh sprigs any time. For drying, cut just before flowering.

SAGE

Use sparingly in sandwich spreads and to flavor stuffings for meat and fowl. Plant about six inches apart in well-drained, light soil. Plant either seeds or cuttings and keep in a moist sunny spot. Cut leaves long before plant flowers; can be used fresh or hung in shade until dry. Cut back plant after it stops blooming.

SUMMER SAVORY

Use to flavor vegetables and fresh or dried in egg or cheese dishes. Plant seeds about six inches apart. It will reach 18 inches and makes a great pot plant, in a sunny location and light dry soil. Cut leaves when plants are in bud and hang them in shade until dry.

TARRAGON

Use in salads, sauces, chicken dishes and to make your own herb vinegar. Plant divided clumps or cuttings of this perennial about one foot apart in a warm sunny spot. Good for hanging basket or must be tightly trained since it spreads quickly. Maximum height will be 12 to 24 inches. Use young tarragon leaves and stem tips any time; loses flavor when dried.

THYME

Use to flavor shellfish, many meats and mixed dishes. Grow in light, well-drained soil or taste is diminished. Grow this shrubby perennial in six-inch pots or in benches in a sunny location. Cut leafy tops and flower clusters when blossoms open and hang them to dry.

Once you have experimented with these herbs, you'll want to try some of the others: garlic (what can we say about that?), caraway (one of our greatest kicks was harvesting and pouring the seeds right into our homemade rye bread dough), chervil, bay leaf (laurel) and horehound. Herbs are fascinating things. When you don't use them, you don't miss them and that's all there is to it. But once you start to use them, you want to use them more and more for the special flavors they impart to your cooking. There's a whole herb world waiting for you out there.

flowering plants for your house

Guests are coming for dinner. For a table centerpiece you choose the delicate, pastel shades of a begonia at the peak of perfect bloom. A few weeks later, the vibrant hues of geranium flowers in softball-size clusters light up your living room. The next week your family delights in the spectacular colors of primrose in combinations that are breathtaking. And still later, the random speckling of pocketbook plants in unique, fascinating-to-see-and-touch shapes sparkle from the kitchen table at supper each night. Different, wonderful, exciting flowering plants you can grow and enjoy, in your greenhouse and in your home all year long.

That's the way it should be done. Grow the plants under the controlled conditions in your greenhouse until they are just ready to burst into flowers, then move them into your home where they can "star" in perfect bloom for days or even weeks.

When you tire of them or they begin to fade, it's back into the greenhouse to rest and prepare for next year's show. For you, it's simply a matter of choosing the next one in bloom to please the eyes and senses of your family.

Of course, all of these plants can be taken out of the greenhouse and placed or planted outside during the proper season. Be sure to bring them back inside quite a bit before the possibility of first frost.

Sounds lovely and easy doesn't it? It is both, but first and foremost it's a matter of doing some homework. How do you grow all these plants in one greenhouse? What if they like different growing conditions? What about temperature ranges? How about light and humidity?

Keeping in mind that plants were not meant to grow indoors, there are ways to solve all these problems. Your greenhouse, with its carefully controlled environment, is the closest thing we can produce indoors to rival a plant's natural habitat. By choosing selectively and intelligently, by matching the environment in your greenhouse to the requirements of a group of plants, you can successfully grow a wide variety of beautiful, flowering plants "indoors."

CAVEAT EMPTOR FOR SURE

A word about buying plants. In this area, as in so many others, the buyer must do his or her homework before going to shop. You should know certain things about plants when choosing them so that you are neither fooled nor "taken."

At most long-established, reputable nurseries, you'll have no trouble selecting plants which are healthy and well bred. In addition, on the more expensive plants, a few of the better nurseries offer a six-month, money-back or exchange guarantee if the plant fails to grow.

However, you should know what to look for, how to help yourself so your own knowledge will provide a personal guarantee of value and quality when you buy potted plants.

• Check to see if the plant matches your knowledge of the variety or the descriptions, which follow this text.

• Be sure the plant looks sturdy and appears to have been tended with knowledge and care.

AFTER BLOOMING IS OVER, SET POT IN A SHADY OUTDOOR SPOT

SINK POT INTO SOIL UP TO RIM

TO KEEP OUT WORMS, MAKE A CAP FOR THE POT BOTTOM OUT OF A LEG OF NYLON HOSE

flowering plants

- Lots of leaves do not necessarily mean the plant is healthy. Look carefully to make sure they are not curled, green not yellowish, but the right size and without any browning, especially at the edges.
- Sparse leaves and skinny, leggy plants usually mean the plant was overfertilized to stimulate fast growth. You want a solid, stocky, well-leaved plant.
- Make sure no roots are growing out of the drainage holes. This usually means the roots are overcrowded in the pot and may be damaged.
- Check all over the plant to be sure you are not getting any insects free of charge along with the plant. And, speaking of insects, after buying, quarantine all newly purchased plants for two weeks until you are certain there are no unwanted guests. Introducing new plants into a greenhouse, without first quarantining, can be disastrous. A cool protected deck or porch, or shaded garden spot out of wind's harm will make a holding place.

The following are some flowering plants you should try in your greenhouse. We have grouped them according to preferred nighttime temperature (cool greenhouse first, moderate greenhouse second) to make your selection process a bit easier. In all cases, the popular name is given first, followed where necessary, by the Latin botanical name, to make identification universally possible.

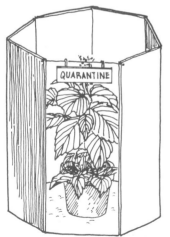

ISOLATE NEW PLANTS
FOR TWO WEEKS BEFORE
PUTTING IN GREENHOUSE
TO BE SURE THEY'RE
NOT BUG-CONTAGIOUS

flowering plants for the cool greenhouse

BEGONIA

To pick your favorite from this family could be a lifetime's work. There are probably more different kinds of begonias for growing as house plants than any other flowering plant. Here is a brief description of the three types: Wax begonias have many small flowers in pink, red or white that grow in front of waxy green or red-green leaves. Rex begonias have small white or pink hanging flowers and very large, handsome leaves shaped like elephant ears. The flowers of tuberous-rooted begonias are about 4 inches across and come in shades of white, pink, red and yellow.

Growing begonias calls for some specialized attention, but results make it all worthwhile. For one thing, plants grown from tubers insist on a rest period. Do not be alarmed when a glorious camellia-like blossoming begonia starts to deteriorate despite all that rich soil and regular feedings. Once cool weather starts, store the sad pot in a cool dark corner, keeping the tuber (not the soil) barely moist. Tuberous begonias are basically outdoor shade plants so don't count on long indoor display.

Wax begonias thrive in morning sunlight, but keep away from midday heat and glare. Rex begonias must be kept shaded. All do best in cool night temperatures of about 55°F and day temperatures in the 70°F range. Wax begonias do best when soil dries between watering and the others like to have damp soil. All like humidity, at least 50 percent, and they do better in clay pots because rapid evaporation keeps roots cool. Feed every two weeks when growing. Always remove all dead flowers, and pinch back foliage to prevent plants from getting "leggy."

TO PROPAGATE,
PIN DOWN A
BEGONIA LEAF,
WITH KNIFE CUTS
ON MAIN RIBS,
WHERE IT WILL ROOT

BELLFLOWER *(Campanula)*

Loads of white or purple-blue flowers appear on trailing stems to make the bellflower a natural for hanging baskets. Improved varieties of old favorites are easy to grow and especially lovely to view.

flowering plants

The bellflower needs at least four to six hours of direct sunlight each day, but must be protected by gauze or a curtain during hottest summer months. Pot up in strong alkaline soil with gravel base to insure good drainage. Water thoroughly and fertilize monthly when growing. Stop feeding and allow to get a bit dry at other times of the year. This plant does best in night temperatures of about 50° to 55°F, and daytime temperatures no higher than 75°F. Start new plants from stem cuttings each spring.

BIRD OF PARADISE *(Strelitzia)*

You'll need lots of patience with these, but it is really worth it. The plant takes 10 years from seed, up to three years from divisions, to produce the fantastic blue and gold exotic bird's head flowers. Foot-long, spear-shaped leaves add to the effect.

Bird of paradise likes at least four to six hours of sunlight each day. Night temperatures about 55°F and daytime temperatures up to 75°F bring out the best in this plant. Grow in standard soil mix, with a bit of extra sand added, in large pots or tubs. Water thoroughly on a wet-dry cycle when growing, then slacken off in the dormant period. Feed every other week during growth.

BLOOD LILY *(Haemanthus)*

These can only be described as spectacular: a flower cluster of red spikes measuring up to 9 inches across sticking into what appears to be a pincushion, sitting atop a slender shaft of 10 to 20 inches. Completing the picture are large leaves surrounding the base of the plant.

Grow these bulb flowers in rich soil that has been laced with sand for extra drainage. Keep in direct sunlight for at least five hours each day. Nighttime temperatures should not move far out of the 50° to 55°F range and daytime temperatures should be at least 70°F. Use a pot that is about two inches larger, all around, than the bulb, and place the bulb so the tip just sticks above the soil.

After flowering, reduce and then stop water and food during

winter. Do not repot too often; once every four or five years is ideal to produce the most profuse flowering. To propagate remove small bulbs growing beside the larger one during rest period; plant one to a pot.

CAMELLIA

These Asian natives are easy to grow, yet react quickly to changes in their environment. Despite that, they are well worth growing for their marvelous, waxy flowers in red, pink and white. Unless you prune camellias they'll outgrow your greenhouse, so clip them and keep them to about three feet in height after blooming is complete.

Plant in soil rich in organic matter. Grow in bright, filtered sunlight in temperatures that range between 45°F at night to about 65° to 70°F during the day. Give plenty of water—in soil (two parts peat moss, one part potting soil and one part sharp sand), in air, on leaves. Feed with acid-type fertilizer every other month starting in early spring. Most problems come from too little humidity, dried-out soil or rapid temperature fluctuation. These conditions will cause buds to drop. A little extra care and you will be rewarded with several weeks of beautiful blooms worthy of any contest.

FLOWERING MAPLE *(Abutilon)*

The less room you give these plants, the more flowers you will get. Keep the plants with their maple-like leaves and bell-shaped flowers pot bound and you will have many, many beautiful blooms in white, salmon, yellow or purple. For the greenhouse your best bet is to select from among the bushy varieties. If you have the room, you might enjoy trying the long, long trailers.

Abutilon is easy to grow if you give it about five hours of sunlight each day, lots of water and food each month. Night temperatures should be about 50°F and daytime temperatures in the 70°F range. Start new plants from new growth clippings you collect when you snip and clip to keep it from taking over the entire greenhouse.

flowering plants

FUCHSIA

Sometimes called "lady's eardrops," these plants are available in trailing or upright varieties. The flowers come in crimson, pink or white, or combinations of the colors, and look like fat, round bells or old-fashioned hoop skirts. Some varieties bloom from summer through fall; others bloom all year long.

Grow in sunshine, but protect from the direct rays of the sun during midsummer heat. Keep the soil evenly moist when growing and feed every two weeks. Night temperature should stay in the 50° to 55°F range and move up as high as 70°F in the daytime. After blooming, cut back into bushier shape, repot, allow to rest for about two months and start all over. Propagate from cuttings of new growth.

GERANIUM *(Pelargonium)*

There are so many different kinds of geraniums available you can pick and choose until you find exactly what you want. For example, old-fashioned people can grow the old-fashioned zonals with the "zone" of brown-green on the leaves. Patriots can grow Martha Washingtons with their beautifully veined leaves and flowers in blends of several colors. Ivy Leaguers can try the ivy-leaved types and swingers can try the carefree types, to name just a few.

Although the preferences of each type of geranium differ a bit from the others, all like night temperatures around 55°F and daytime temperatures around 65°F. Water when soil is moderately dry and feed every other week until October. Give plenty of direct sunshine. Slacken off on both water and food after blooms are gone. Start new plants from stem cuttings any time. Try as many kinds as you can. They are different, fun and easy to grow.

HELIOTROPE *(Heliotropium)*

A little of their fragrance goes a very long way. New varieties of these old-time favorites have been improved and are available in several blue-purple shades as well as in white. One plant covered with clusters of these tiny flowers is enough to give a beautiful fragrance to a large home and any greenhouse.

Grow in direct sunlight and temperatures that range from 50°F at night to about 70°F during the day. Water thoroughly and frequently and feed every other week. Keep trained to bushy form and use cuttings to start new plants.

MEXICAN FLAME VINE *(Senecio)*

There's a whole species of colorful flowers available called *Senecio.* The Mexican flame vine *(Senecio confusus)* has deep orange, daisy-type flowers which appear several times each year. Parlor or German ivy *(Senecio mikanioides)* has much smaller yellow flowers that fall into pretty clusters. A third sister, cineraria *(Senecio cruentus),* has large clusters of deeply colored, velvet-textured, daisylike flowers of red, blue, purple or pink, with white centers for some.

The whole group likes at least four hours of direct sunlight throughout the summer months and as much as they can get for the remainder of the year. Cinerarias like filtered summer sun and cooler temperatures than the others—50°F at night, 65°F in the daytime. Other *Senecio* prefer it about five degrees warmer all day and all night. Give all frequent watering and fertilize once each month. Keep all pinched back, particularly after flowering; try growing cuttings.

POCKETBOOK PLANT *(Calceolaria)*

These must be seen to be believed and appreciated. Loads of puffed-up, pouch-like blossoms growing above large, dark-green leaves. Pocketbook plants come in a great many colors—shades of red, pink, violet, yellow, maroon, with specks of other colors thrown in as well.

Somewhat more difficult to grow than other plants, these beauties like light porous soil, shade, cool temperatures at night (40° to 45°F) and daytime temperatures about 60°F. Water when soil is dry and stop food when blossoms appear; otherwise, keep soil moist and feed weekly during growing period. Start seed in fall for spring blooms.

flowering plants

SHOOTING STAR *(Cyclamen)*

These Mediterranean natives are considered to be among the prettiest plants around. Marvelous red, white or pink flowers seem to shoot through masses of heart-shaped, white- or silver-marked leaves on slender stems.

Keep these plants in bright light where temperatures go no higher than 60°F during the day. Nighttime temperatures should be on the cool side, 40° to 50°F. When plant is blooming, keep evenly moist and fertilize every other week. After flowering has stopped, allow soil to dry out, remove tuber and put into cool storage. In the fall repot so half the tuber is above the soil, half below.

SHRIMP PLANT *(Beloperone)*

It just takes one look to see where this got its name. The hanging white flowers growing out of reddish-colored bracts do look like shrimp. Other varieties come in yellow, red and combinations of red and yellow, all with hairy pea-green leaves that sometimes grow as long as the bracts.

These colorful Mexican natives bloom all year long if they receive at least five hours of sunlight each day. They do best in cool temperatures at night (about 50°F) and warm temperatures all day (up to about 75°F). Water thoroughly and then allow the soil to become almost dry before watering again. Feed every two weeks. To keep the plant from becoming scraggly and ungainly, pinch off stem tips when the plants are about one foot long. Use the pinched off tips to start new plants.

SWEET ALYSSUM *(Lobularia)*

These tiny little plants, covered with clusters of miniature flowers in white, pink and purple, look marvelous in teacups and are a must for any greenhouse. Grow them and then spot them around your home at bloom time and you'll certainly have a winner.

Grow from seed in direct sunlight and watch them sprout in only a few days. Keep the soil moist, feed about once each month, and maintain night temperatures about 55°F and day temperatures at least 70°F. They enjoy additional humidity, too. Sow enough for yourself and to give as delicate, long-lasting gifts.

YESTERDAY-TODAY-AND-TOMORROW *(Brunfelsia)*

Also known as "kiss-me-quick," these plants do a slow-change act. On the first day of bloom the flowers are purple, on the second day lavender and on the third day white. Since the flowers do their thing in turn, it always appears as if the plant has blooms in the various colors.

Keep these slightly pot bound in highly organic soil, one part peat moss to one of soil. Give at least four or five hours of bright, filtered sunlight and temperatures that range from 55°F at night to well over 70°F—in the warm zone of your greenhouse—during the day. The soil should be thoroughly and evenly moist at all times; feed every other week. Cut back on water and food when plant is resting. Clip plant to keep it compact, then use the tips to make new plants.

flowering plants for the moderate greenhouse

AMARYLLIS *(Hippeastrum)*

Tall, stately and magnificent is the best and easiest way to identify the South African amaryllis. Huge, 10-inch white, pink or red blooms sitting atop stiff two-foot-tall, arrow-straight shafts. You'll only really appreciate these when you have grown them yourself.

Plant a single bulb to a pot allowing about two inches between bulb and pot wall. Position the bulb so about half remains above soil level. Water thoroughly, then withhold water until stem appears. Start watering and feeding slowly again as bud appears. Keep in sunny spot where temperatures are about 60°F at night and at least 70°F during the day, but out of direct sunlight when in bloom.

When leaves yellow, stop watering. Move to cool spot and store for several months. Start anew and watch for wonderful blooms. Bulblets will form next to large bulb; use these to start new plants.

103

BY CHANGING A WINDOW OR DOOR YOU
CAN WALK RIGHT INTO A GREENHOUSE
ATTACHED TO THE LIVING STRUCTURE
—A PLACE TO ENJOY BREAKFAST OR
THE END-OF-DAY HOUR.

BOUGAINVILLEA

Don't let these tropical beauties get away from you. Unpinched and unpruned, these vines tend to want to take over the world. Prune carefully and train to a support or other trellis. Choose a height that suits you (two to 15 feet) and keep the plant to that height. This is another plant with bracts that are prettier than the flowers. No matter, enjoy the red, pink, purple, copper and white "flowers" whatever they are called.

Also called "paper flowers," bougainvilleas like warm weather, so keep nighttime temperatures around 60° to 65°F and day temperatures no more than 10 degrees higher. Water thoroughly during growing season; allow to become almost dry at other times. Provide ample sun for bloom. Feed every two weeks as the plants grow and bloom, then stop for a rest period. Start new plants from stem cuttings in spring.

CARDINAL PLANT *(Rechsteineria)*

These tropical Brazilian beauties have close relatives called Brazilian edelweiss. Both are quite pretty. The cardinal has lovely red, tubular flowers; the edelweiss has flowers that are closer to a rosy-salmon color. The leaves of the cardinal plant are heart-shaped, about five inches long and quite hairy or almost woody.

Grow the tubers in bright summer light or direct winter sun in soil that has an extra measure of peat moss. Keep in nighttime temperatures of almost 70°F and about five degrees higher during the daylight hours. Water only when soil becomes dry to the touch and do it from the bottom so no water spills on the leaves. Feed once a month during the growing season and not at all the rest of the year.

COLUMNEA

Very long, very showy hanging plants are what you get with these easy-to-grow tropical natives. Give plenty of indirect bright light, water (add extra peat moss to soil mix to retain moisture) and a once-a-month feeding. You'll watch them grow and grow and grow. Warmth and

flowering plants

humidity are the bywords with these plants, so keep night temperatures at about 65°F and daytime temperatures more than 10 degrees higher.

Select from very showy flowers of red, orange or yellow with contrasting throats and hairs. To make the plant bushier and prettier, prune after each flowering period. Use the cuttings to make new plants.

CRAPE-JASMINE *(Ervatamia)*

Also called butterfly gardenias, these plants look like true gardenias, especially at a quick, first glance. The shiny, dark-green leaves act as a perfect backdrop for the delightfully scented, large white flowers. Blooms appear all summer long and occasionally during the remainder of the year.

Keep these plants in at least five hours of strong, direct sunlight each day and temperatures of 65°F at night and over 75°F all day long. Water often and thoroughly so soil is always moist. During growing season fertilize every other week and once each month for the remainder of the year. Prune carefully to keep plants to desired shape and size. Use cuttings to make new plants.

CROSSANDRA

These are especially appealing because with proper care they will bloom all year long. Natives of the East Indies, these plants grow to about one foot tall and have large salmon-orange flowers.

Plant in regular potting soil mix with a bit of extra peat moss added. Keep the plants in at least four hours of sunshine each day, but protect from sun's direct rays during the summer. They only need a temperature difference of five degrees, from night to day, from 65° to 70°F. Keep the soil moist at all times, mist the plant frequently and fertilize every two weeks with a liquid plant food all year round. Remove old blossoms weekly to encourage bloom. Start new plants from cuttings or seed sown in perlite or sand.

FIRECRACKER VINE *(Manettia)*

You know, they really do look like miniature firecrackers. The blooms appear all year long, and are firecracker red with yellow tips, one inch long and tubular in shape. Because the plant is a vine, you can train it on a trellis or other support for compact enjoyment.

Grow these interesting and attractive plants in light shade and be sure the soil remains moist at all times. Night temperatures should be about 55°F and daytime temperatures at least 70°F. Feed every two weeks throughout the year. Use stem cuttings for new plants; young plants bloom best so start new ones every year.

FLAME VIOLET *(Episcia)*

Treat these tropical Americans as you do African violets and they will in turn treat you to beautiful marked leaves and pretty white, pink, yellow, orange or red flowers, in spring and summer.

Pot in peat moss-enriched soil that is kept moist, and feed every other week during the growing season. Don't allow temperatures to drop below 55°F or the leaves will turn black. Daytime temperatures higher than 75°F are ideal, and 50 to 75 percent humidity. Clip plants after blooming period so they don't look straggly and use cuttings to start new plants. They have no dormant period without leaves.

FLAMINGO FLOWER *(Anthurium)*

Grow these in your greenhouse and it will look like the true stereotype of a greenhouse—a tropical forest. Your warm greenhouse will do well for these Central American plants because they like warmth, moisture, high humidity and light.

Grow in pots of pure sphagnum moss or fir bark (no soil) that is kept constantly moist. To get the droopy, tail-like spadices to bloom throughout the year, keep the plant where it gets lots of filtered sunlight. Add liquid plant food once each month. Keep night temperatures in the 60°F range and daytime temperatures at least 70°F. A little bit of extra care and pampering will get you plants that are interesting

flowering plants

to grow and fascinating to see. You can start new plants from the small side shoots.

GARDENIA

Try one of these magnificently fragrant plants if you like a challenge. Gardenias are a bit fussier than many other flowering plants, but treated right they will treat you to large, beautiful waxy flowers that can measure up to three inches across.

Give these plants at least four or five hours of direct sunlight each day. Keep the soil moist and acidy by enriching with peat moss. When buds are forming, fertilize with acid food every two weeks and cut back to once a month at other times. Mist foliage daily to insure the necessary humidity and cut down on bud-drop, particularly when you bring the gardenia indoors.

Temperature can be critical. Day temperatures around 70°F are ideal. At night, at least a five-degree drop is essential. If temperature rises above 65°F at night, new flower buds will probably not set.

GLOXINIA *(Sinningia)*

See these Brazilian beauties in full bloom and you'll know you have to grow them no matter what else has to go. The bell-shaped flowers that grow from three to six inches across come in white, pink, red and purple, various shades of each, frequently edged, spotted and outlined with contrasting colors. All of this color stands tall above large, velvet leaves that act as support and gorgeous background.

Gloxinias do best in generous light, but no direct sunlight which would shrivel leaves; too-low light makes them leggy and the leaves will curl. Pot the tuber, covering completely with only new sprout exposed, in soil that has extra peat moss. Water thoroughly and regularly when plant is growing, keeping the water away from the leaves. Feed with African violet-type fertilizer once a month. After that, cut back and then stop watering. When new sprouts appear in several months, repot, water, fertilize and get ready for more gorgeous blooms.

HIBISCUS

At least 25 years of continuous bloom is what you can expect from the easy-to-grow, beautiful Chinese hibiscus. The flowers are paper-like and mature at a terrific five inches across. They can be had in shades of white, cream, yellow, pink, salmon and red—each one prettier than the next one.

The plants grow very tall if left alone, but you can and should keep them to about four feet with careful pruning. Use the pruned branches (that have woody stems) to start new plants. Simply stick them in moist sand or vermiculite for rooting. Hibiscus needs plenty of room for roots to keep plentiful bloom.

Give your hibiscus at least four hours of direct sunlight each day, soil with good drainage, lots of water and fertilizer once a month. Daytime temperatures of 70°F or higher and nighttime temperatures around 60°F are ideal.

LANTANA

You call the shots here. Which do you prefer—a hanging plant, a pot plant or one that grows on a standard? Careful pruning and training give you exactly what you want with these versatile tropical plants. Flowers come in white, yellow, pink, red, orange and multicolor combinations among rough-textured, strong-smelling leaves.

These are fast growers that need plenty of direct sunshine and temperatures of about 60°F at night and about 70°F during the day. Water only when the soil feels dry to the touch. Feed every three weeks. Use clippings, made while pruning, to start new plants.

LIPSTICK PLANT *(Aeschyanthus)*

Once seen, it doesn't require much imagination to understand why these Java natives are not only called lipstick plant but basket vine as well. Since the vines grow to a length of about four feet, there will be plenty of colorful lipsticks to see and enjoy. If you prefer, with careful pruning you can keep them shorter.

flowering plants

Though they like some sunlight, lipstick plants do best in bright light that has been filtered to stop direct, burning rays. Grow in a soil mixture that has extra peat moss to hold the additional moisture you'll need to supply; never let them dry out and add moisture by misting. Fertilize once each month. These plants love warmth; give them about 70°F at night and at least 75°F during the day.

MAGIC FLOWER *(Achimenes)*

Another relative of the African violet, these plants reward growers with an abundance of pretty, satin-shiny flowers from early spring to late fall. The flowers look a bit like tiny petunias and come in white, pink, blue, red, rose and violet, most often with a contrasting color throat. Check on the kind you are getting. Some trail and are fine for hanging baskets, while others grow upright.

True to their Central American ancestry, these plants like ample filtered sunlight, warm days (75°F) and nights (65°F), moist soil (a mixture of peat moss, perlite and leaf mold) and food about once a month. After bloom has gone, stop watering to allow rhizome to go dormant. Store rhizomes in a plastic bag in a 60°F spot and repot in the spring.

PASSION FLOWER *(Passiflora)*

These vine flowers with the mystical center crown must be seen to be believed. Native to Brazil, the flowers grow to four or five inches across in white, pink, purple and combinations of each, and cling, by tendrils, to whatever is near. Train these carefully up a support or trellis or, for a fantastic display, allow to grow along some greenhouse supports or around a venting window.

Start this plant in a large tub of potting soil so there is plenty of room for spreading roots. Put the tub where it will get at least five hours of direct sunlight each day. Give lots of water, fertilize every two weeks during growing season and watch it take off.

Nighttime temperatures should be about 60°F and daytime temperatures should be at least 10 degrees warmer. Allow the plant to rest in winter in dry soil and in a 55°F location. Cut back to six inches in January to encourage branching, and plant up cuttings.

PATIENT LUCY *(Impatiens)*

This Lucy is fun to watch, although a bit messy. When seed pods become ripe they explode shooting seeds all over the place. A favorite with young and old alike, *Impatiens* will grow and bloom without too much fuss and bother on your part. Choose from varieties with white, pink, coral, purple or combination-color flowers and leaves accented with white or maroon.

Natives of East Africa, *Impatiens* do best when they get ample amounts of bright light and water and bi-monthly applications of plant food. They droop noticeably as soon as water is needed. Use extra peat moss in the potting mix to help retain moisture in soil. Frequent pinching back will give you starts for new plants. Root cuttings in moist, coarse sand. Temperatures around 60°F at night and at least 70°F all day are what they like best.

TEMPLE BELLS *(Smithiantha)*

These popular plants come from Guatemala and Mexico, bringing with them pretty flowers and fascinating foliage. The leaves are heart-shaped, deep green, marbled with red and covered with velvety red hair. The flowers, shaped like bells, come in pink, red, yellow, orange or white, with accent spots and streaks inside in contrasting colors.

Grow in filtered sunlight and high humidity. These plants like nighttime temperatures of about 70°F and daytime temperatures at least five degrees higher.

After bloom, allow soil to almost dry and keep in a cool spot, where rhizomes can rest two to three months. Divide the rhizomes, pot up in African violet soil in four-inch pots, and you'll soon be on your way to beautiful blooms and, this time around . . . even more of them. If they seem to grow slowly, they probably need more warmth.

blooming times for greenhouse flowers

By starting your plants from seeds, bulbs or cuttings you can control the blooming time and with careful planning be assured of year-round blossoms in your greenhouse. The charts below indicate how long it will be before you can expect flowers after planting the seeds or cuttings.

COOL GREENHOUSE FLOWERS

Flower: Started From	Will Bloom In
Begonia, tuberous, Seed	6 months
Begonia, wax, Seed	6 months
Bellflower, Cuttings	1 year
Bird of paradise, Division	3 years
Blood lily, Bulbs	6-9 months
Camellia, Cuttings	2 years
Seed	3-4 years
Flowering maple, Cuttings	4 months
Fuchsia, Cuttings	8 months
Geranium, Cuttings	6 months
Heliotrope, Cuttings	6 months
Mexican flame vine, Seed	7 months
Pocketbook plant, Seed	8 months
Shooting star, Seed	18 months
Shrimp plant, Cuttings	8 months
Sweet alyssum, Seed	5 months
Yesterday, etc., Cuttings	9 months

MODERATE GREENHOUSE FLOWERS

Flower: Started From	Will Bloom In
Amaryllis, Bulbs	4 months
Bougainvillea, Cuttings	9 months
Cardinal plant, Seed	1 year
Columnea, Cuttings	6 months
Crape-jasmine, Cuttings	8 months
Crossandra, Cuttings	3 months
Firecracker vine, Cuttings	6 months
Flame violet, Cuttings	1 year
Flamingo flower, Seed	2 years
Gardenia, Cuttings	18 months
Gloxinia, Seed	7 months
Tubers	5 months
Hibiscus, Cuttings	9 months
Lantana, Cuttings	6 months
Lipstick plant, Cuttings	1 year
Magic flower, Division	6 months
Passion flower, Cuttings	6 months
Patient Lucy, Cuttings	3 months
Temple bells, Division	6 months

unusual blooming plants

FAREWELL-TO-SPRING *(Godetia)*

Also known as the satin flower for its lovely flowers of rose, purple or white, these plants must have cool weather. Start seeds in late September. A good growing temperature of 50° to 55°F will produce mature flowering plants, one to two feet tall in four months. These are spring and summer annuals, so discard after flowering.

PAINTED TONGUE *(Salpiglossis)*

Name comes from Greek, *salpinx* (trumpet), *glossa* (tongue), and aptly describes the large funnel-shaped flowers of this annual. Shades of yellow, scarlet, blue, purple and violet are yours to choose. Plant reaches a height of one to three feet and will need to be discarded after flowering, which takes place in five to six months. Start seeds in a loose potting mix in peat pots; keep warm, moist. When seedlings appear in a week, thin out to one to a pot. As they grow, pinch out tips to force branching. Painted tongue makes a great cut flower for bouquets.

WINDFLOWER *(Anemone japonica)*

The name is said to come from the Greek *anemos*, wind. That's a real misnomer because these flowers do not like the wind and when grown outdoors need to be in a sheltered spot. Choose from white, rose, red, pink or lavender. The mature height of these hardy perennials is six to 18 inches and they flower in three to five months, from the time new growth appears each year. These are fibrous-rooted, which grow slowly, but readily, if roots are not disturbed. You can divide roots in fall or early spring. If you are the pioneer type and prefer to plant seeds, start them in the autumn. Seeds will take one year to mature and bloom. Once started windflowers like full sun and growing temperatures of about 60°F. Propagate mature plants by division in September.

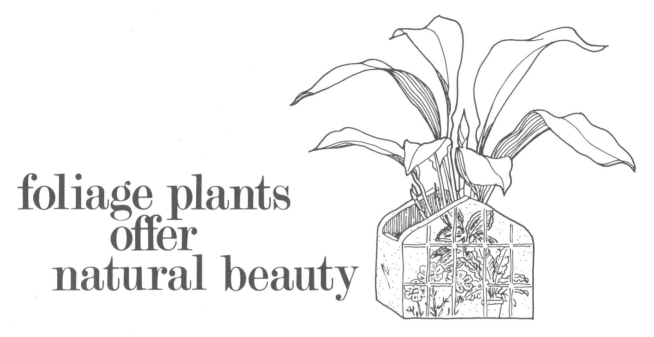

foliage plants offer natural beauty

No one will ever know how it happened, that momentous day when a nature lover, or more accurately a plant lover, took that first outdoor plant indoors. We also don't know if those first efforts were a success or a failure (lucky for that gardener, no one likes to have failures recorded to live on and on). We do know, though, that it had to be difficult. Plants were never intended to be grown indoors in a foreign, even hostile, environment.

Think of the "impossibilities." There wasn't enough light for some plants, too much for others. Some indoor spots were too hot, others too dry, too cold or too wet. The only greenery was on slipcovers, or an occasional *Aspidistra.* Of course, we now have it easy. Over the years indoor gardeners have not only learned how to grow the plants that require certain growing conditions, but even how to change those conditions if they are wrong. Now, in our houses and apartments we can add or subtract light, raise or lower moisture levels, keep the air warm and sultry as a tropical jungle, or cool as the proverbial cucumber. This kind of knowledge, experimentation, trial and error and years of experience has opened the doors wide to all sorts of gardening.

foliage plants

Many of us live in imposed environments where we can't change light or temperature or humidity to please an exotic green for which we have a yen. Or, we are frustrated by lack of space for big foliage—or a place to start cuttings without cluttering a kitchen countertop. Now doors to new, exciting and economical greenhouses magically open to give space for ideal plant living, for indulging in all the variety of magnificent and unbelievable growables, from pinkie-nail tiny to umbrella-large.

The following are very special foliage plants we think you should try in your greenhouse, and move in and out of your home as you like. Again, we have divided them according to the kind of greenhouse, giving first cool, then moderate. These are, of course, just a sampling to get you started. Read the descriptions and try the ones that appeal to you most. Try some, then try some more. Keep brief notes on the treatment you give each plant. Experiment to come up with the winningest combination of foliage for you.

Be careful though. You may be surprised to discover foliage plants are addictive. Every time you walk into a nursery you will see something new, something different, something you've "got to have." It seems astounding that there can be so many different kinds. But if that does happen to you ... good. It has happened to us. We go slightly crazy each time we walk through our local nurseries. Why should we be the only ones to have this wonderful "problem"? Join us! You'll love it.

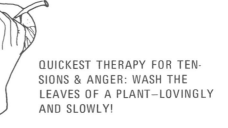

QUICKEST THERAPY FOR TENSIONS & ANGER: WASH THE LEAVES OF A PLANT—LOVINGLY AND SLOWLY!

foliage plants

foliage plants for the cool greenhouse

CAST IRON PLANT *(Aspidistra)*

It truly is just about cast iron; this long-time favorite will do well under almost impossible conditions. *Aspidistra* will even survive if temperatures are too high, the air too dry and the light very poor. But, remember, that is only survival.

To get the best out of these wonderful plants from China, keep them where they are in light shade, with temperatures of about 50°F at night and at least 70°F during the day. Feed them about once a month except during fall and winter, and water so the soil is slightly moist.

When these lovely foliage plants are well cared for you can have two-and-a-half-foot-tall plants with shiny, arching, almost black-green leaves (from one variety) and green-and-white-striped or spotted leaves (from another). To make many new plants from the one you have, divide the roots and pot in a packaged general-purpose soil mix.

GOLD DUST TREE *(Aucuba)*

Few of us get to see gold, much less select how we want to find it. With this plant we can choose leaves speckled all over with gold dust, or edged in dark green with golden-yellow centers, or the reverse—green centers and golden-yellow edges. *Aucuba* makes us all King Midas.

To bring out their golden spots, give gold dust trees ample time in bright but not direct sunlight. And watch the temperatures; coolness is the word. About 45°F at night and about 65°F during the day is the comfort range most appreciated by these decorative, large-leaved trees. Water only enough to keep the soil moist but not wet; they relish extra humidity, too. Feed no more than three times each year.

IVY *(Hedera)*

This plant is terrific to grow because of the wide variety of interesting, unusual leaf shapes, colors, sizes and textures from which you may choose. They can also be grown and trained in different ways, as topiary or as trailers to name but two. Look for various shades of green, the specialty species and the ones with either delicate or bold markings. All are very attractive, worth trying and need relatively little care.

Ivies grow fantastically when they get plenty of direct sunlight, but will do reasonably well in bright indirect light. Pot in regular soil mix that is kept moist but not wet. Wash the leaves frequently with clear water to keep them fresh-looking and to discourage mites and aphids.

Night temperatures of about 50°F and day temperatures around 70°F are fine, and yet the "easy-going" ivies will also do well in even greater temperature extremes. Pinch off stems to create a bushy plant and, as a bonus, use the "pinchings" to make new plants.

LAUREL *(Laurus)*

Here's something that might surprise you: Laurel leaves are the bay leaves we use in cooking. Fresh bay leaves add a superb flavor to food, but are quite strong; use sparingly.

Drafts will be no problem to this slow-growing plant, so you can put them where more tender plants fear to grow. Give them direct sunlight, moist soil with peat moss and sand added and food every other month until August and you'll have a winner. Night temperatures of about 40°F and day temperatures no higher than about 65°F are best. Taking stem cuttings will keep the plant bushy and provide you with materials for new plants as well.

NORFOLK ISLAND PINE *(Araucaria)*

That's right. Norfolk pine, a tree, a real tree, will grow in your greenhouse. It looks like a Christmas tree. Bring it out of the greenhouse into your home and decorate it for the holidays. In its native New Zealand, this tree can grow to about 200 feet in height. In your greenhouse it will probably reach your height and then call it quits.

These marvelous pine trees do best in lots of light, but not in direct sunlight. They prefer cool night temperatures of about 50°F and day temperatures of at least 74°F. Keep the soil mixture (highly organic,

foliage plants

like African violets) just about moist and feed only about three times each year. Repot only at three- or four-year intervals. If your plant loses its wonderful, balanced shape, check the amount of light it is getting. With little light, this pine reacts with uneven growth.

OLIVE *(Olea)*

Even back in Biblical days they talked often about these trees. Though the olive has only a few, tiny white flowers and almost no chance of fruit, it makes a lovely gray-green foliage plant when grown in the greenhouse.

Grow in full sunlight and give water only when soil (leaf mold and sand added to loam) becomes dry to the touch. Feed with a 5-10-5 fertilizer twice a year and prune frequently to give this bushy green a tree shape indoors that will lift it above low-foliage plants. Use the tip cuttings to start new trees.

Although the olive can withstand rather low temperatures during its dormant period, try not to let it get below 40°F at night and then warm it up to about 75°F during daylight hours.

PIGGYBACK PLANT *(Tolmiea)*

This is a plant that grows new plants, in miniature, at the base of each leaf. No wonder these plants with hairy, green leaves are also known as "mother of thousands." Natives of western North America, piggyback plants are fun to grow and give as gifts.

Keep these prolific propagators in lots of indirect sunlight. Water thoroughly and frequently, so soil (packaged potting mix is ideal) is kept moist. Add plant food every other month. Cool temperatures are preferred, so keep night temperatures around 50°F and daytime temperatures in the very low 70°F range. Make as many new plants as you desire by simply setting the mature leaves with the new plantlets attached in a pot of soil next to the mother plants, and sever the connection when they root.

PIN A PIGGYBACK (WITH BABIES) IN A SMALL POT WITH HALF A PAPER CLIP; THE LITTLE ONE SHOULD ROOT IN 2 WEEKS, THEN CUT THE CONNECTION

PITTOSPORUM

These decorative variegated green and white natives of Japan grow beautifully, leaving you worry-free. Even drafts don't seem to bother them. Grow in a soil mix of leaf mold, loam and sand, in direct sunlight and water only after soil feels quite dry to the touch. Feed a high-phosphorus diet twice each year, but otherwise ignore them except to look at and enjoy. They tend to grow quite wide and take space, so prune and use cuttings to start new plants.

Will tolerate night temperatures as low as 40°F and day temperatures as high as 80°F.

PODOCARPUS

These shrubby plants can grow tall and skinny to 50 or 60 feet outdoors, but make wonderful indoor foliage plants—if you remember to keep pruning. Aside from cutting back, don't worry about them; just grow and enjoy.

Grow in a sunny spot where there are not too many drafts. This shrub seems to accept wide temperature fluctuations—45°F at night to 85°F during the day. Water to keep soil barely moist and add plant food with a 5-10-5 count only twice each year. Start new plants from stem cuttings in September or October.

SPIDER PLANT (Chlorophytum)

If you are a plant giver or sharer, this is for you. From South Africa, these plants were named for their long, arching leaves and stems which look like long-legged spiders. At the end of these long stems new plantlets develop when simply allowed to touch soil. Couldn't be easier. If you don't root them and instead allow them to hang over the edge of a pot, they will grow bigger and bigger, adding to the cascade effect of the long, thin, green-and-white-striped leaves.

Moisture at all times and lots of indirect light are the steps to success with spider plants. Cool night temperatures of about 50°F and warm day temperatures of about 70°F are best. Feed only three times a

SAVE YOUR BACK—DON'T LIFT HEAVY PLANTS. DRAG THEM, WHEEL THEM, ROLL THEM

foliage plants

year. You can make new plants as often as they appear; longer-light days encourage more "babies."

TREE IVY *(Fatshedera)*
Started as an accidental cross between Japanese *Fatsia* and Irish ivy, tree ivy acquired the best characteristics of both parents—shrubbiness and wonderful foliage. Keep these large-leaved lovelies in a sunny spot, watering only when soil is almost dry, and feed with any acceptable house plant food every three months. Night temperatures should be on the cool side, about 40°F, warming up to about 72°F during daylight hours. Cut back each spring to keep plants healthy and growing compactly. Use cuttings to make new plants. Pot up when rooted in a packaged soil mix.

foliage plants for the moderate greenhouse

ALUMINUM PLANT *(Pilea)*
This quilt-leaf plant looks as if it were marked with aluminum paint—silver gray among the green. Although other close relatives also have interesting foliage, try these first—they are ideally suited for greenhouse growing and offer contrast to the darker big-leaf exotics.

Grow aluminum plants in bright but indirect sunlight. Water as soon as soil seems almost dry to the touch. Feed every other month with well-diluted, water-soluble food. Night temperatures of about 65°F are fine, but warmer days, as high as 85°F, are important. Prune frequently to keep from getting leggy and either use the clippings for new plants, or divide roots and plant in a mixture of equal parts packaged potting soil and peat moss.

CALADIUM
Huge, magnificent, irregular hearts in a wide range of colors are yours when you grow these tropical natives. Some of the leaves measure as much as two feet across and feel almost like fine tissue paper.

Start these from tubers. Press the tubers about one inch deep, with the bud pointed down, into a moist soil mixture of half vermiculite and half peat moss. When leaves appear, repot in a mixture of half packaged soil and half leaf mold. Give the plants plenty of indirect sunlight, moisture and feed every other week. Keep in night temperatures around 65°F and day temperatures around 80° to 85°F.

When leaves start to wither (at least six months after they have appeared), slow down, then stop watering. Knock dead tops and dry soil off tuber and store in dry peat moss at 55°F. Wait about five months, and start again.

CHINESE EVERGREEN *(Aglaonema)*

These Southeast Asian natives are pretty—and pretty hard to kill. If you have any doubts about your gardening ability, start with these. Their indestructibility will build your confidence and your ego. There are quite a few different species of *Aglaonema,* so pick and choose according to leaf shape, texture, color and markings. These plants will not only grow beautifully in soil under almost any conditions, but will also do well grown in water. If you grow them in water, add a few small bits of aquarium charcoal to keep the water sweet.

To be especially nice to these plants, give them very little light, just enough water to keep the soil barely moist and water-soluble fertilizer (5-10-5) three times a year. Night temperatures of about 60°F and daytime temperatures up to 85°F are desirable. Start new plants from stem cuttings, but don't just keep propagating from the same ones. You owe it to yourself to try different species for a variety of wonderful foliage color. If you're lucky, you will find a "partner" who is willing to share cuttings.

COLEUS

Java sends us these colorful plants to brighten any home or greenhouse. And they grow beautifully without much help, in an almost impossible-to-believe number of leaf colors. The great majority are

foliage plants

beautiful combinations of all shades of green, red, maroon, pink and yellow. Occasionally coleus will sprout some very insignificant flowers. When that happens, pinch them off as soon as they appear. You will then have more and more exquisite leaves.

Provide coleus with direct sunlight, enough water to keep the soil just moist and food four times each year and you'll get amazing results. Warm nights, about 70°F, and very warm days, about 85°F, are favored by these plants. Start new plants from cuttings at any time of the year.

CORN PLANT *(Dracaena)*

Does the idea of corn growing in your home or greenhouse strike you as funny? Go ahead and laugh, then plant *Dracaena.* The leaves look just like the leaves of a corn stalk. Because there are so many different varieties in this genus, it is frequently difficult to identify some of its members. The two most popular members of this African native have long, pointed, sword-shaped leaves: one with wide yellow bands down the green leaf, the other with green-and-white bands along the edges. You can also find *Dracaena* with gold spots, yellow stripes and more.

Keep them out of direct sunlight, but give them plenty of daylight. Water thoroughly as soon as the soil starts to get dry and never let plants stand in water. Feed sparingly only twice each year and maintain night temperatures of about 65°F and daytime temperatures up to 85°F. New plants may be made, whenever you wish, by taking cuttings, which root in water.

CROTON *(Codiaeum)*

Close your eyes and pick. These tropical Malaysian natives come in so many varieties, sizes, colors and shapes it is just about impossible to see or try them all. Crotons' fascination is enhanced because no two plants within a single variety are the same and even the leaves on the same plant may have different colors and patterns. Choose from among leaves that are long and thin, flat and wide or twisted like a corkscrew.

Then, of course, there are the colors: yellows, reds, oranges, greens, browns and pinks in solids, spots, stripes and splotches.

To entice them to grow at their colorful best, give crotons at least five hours of direct sunlight each day. Provide just enough moisture to keep them damp, but never let them sit in water. Feed only during their natural growing time (spring and summer) and after that, every two months. Warmth at all times also brings out their best—65° to 70°F at night and at least 80°F during the day.

CUT LEAF OR SPLIT LEAF PHILODENDRON *(Monstera)*

Though they look like *Philodendron*, they are not. These long-popular foliage plants come from Mexico and Guatemala where they grow as parasite vines. In the greenhouse you can either grow them in pots, or on slabs of wood with the bark attached. They are real beauties—large, soft, leather-textured leaves, eight to 18 inches across, on big, healthy-looking plants—and are very easy to grow.

Indirect sunlight is best. Water when soil is dry and add house plant food twice a year and your plants will be happy. Night temperatures of about 65°F and day temperatures about 80°F are excellent, although temperatures above and below don't seem to cause this plant any discomfort.

Make new plants from cuttings. This procedure serves two purposes: It keeps the plant pruned and handsome, and provides new plants from old.

DUMB CANE *(Dieffenbachia)*

Dumb canes are beautiful to look at, but beware. The leaves and stems contain poisons that cause painful swelling of the mouth and tongue, making you dumb temporarily, hence the name. Be especially careful if there are children at home and warn them against touching or handling this plant. Despite this, *Dieffenbachia* are big, popular plants with very large fan-shaped leaves covered with stripes, spots and dabs of white and ivory.

SLOW, COMPLETE WATERING BY IMMERSION DOES THE BEST JOB FOR BIG-LEAF GREENS

foliage plants

No great problem growing them. Just give them ample light but no sunlight, and water thoroughly only after soil has become dry to the touch. Feed four times each year with diluted liquid plant food and keep warm. Day temperatures of about 85°F and night about 70°F will keep the dumb cane thriving. If it gets too tall and has no lower leaves, try air layering to bring it back to manageable size and plant the rooted top at the base of the parent plant.

INDIAN RUBBER TREE *(Ficus)*

Mention this name and everyone knows it, as well as its close relatives, weeping fig *(Ficus benjamina),* and fiddle-leaf fig *(Ficus pandurata). Ficus'* fame is understandable. These trees have been grown successfully by indoor gardeners for years and years and years. Natives of India and Malaysia, Indian rubber trees with their very large, beautiful leaves can become immense—too large for most greenhouses. Careful pruning and training, however, will keep them from growing through the roof.

Grow them in regular potting mixture in a slightly smaller pot than you would normally use for such a big plant. *Ficus* prefer to be a little pot bound, rather than having extra room to wiggle their roots. Keep them in a spot with plenty of bright but not direct sunlight. Water to keep soil just moist except in winter, then allow to dry a bit. Apply plant food sparingly—only once in six months. Warm temperatures are best—nighttime 65° to 70°F, daytime 70° to 85°F. Wash leaves with water frequently. For some unexplained reason many people "polish" these beautiful leaves. *Never* do that. Never polish them or wipe them down with oil or anything else.

Air layering is the best way to get new plants from *Ficus* varieties. If the rubber tree grows too tall, simply cut it back a foot or two and root the cutting in water. A good potting mixture is one part potting soil, one of sharp sand and one of peat moss. The new plant may need a stake until it can support itself.

MOSAIC PLANT *(Fittonia)*

This Peruvian native has a fascinating network of clearly visible red or white veins all over every leaf. Its extraordinary patterning certainly qualifies *Fittonia* as an outstanding foliage plant. Be certain you keep these in the most humid spot in the greenhouse or supply as much humidity as possible. Give plenty of light, but no direct sunlight. Feed once each month using well-diluted liquid fish emulsion fertilizer—no more than half as much as is recommended on the package.

Night temperatures of about 65°F and day temperatures as high as 85°F are fine. Prune to maintain compact shape and make new plants from the cuttings.

PEACOCK PLANT *(Calathea)*

Some people call these "jazzy prayer plants"—for good reason. They are members of the same family as the prayer plant *(Maranta)* and also come from Brazil. The peacocks are very colorful with red stalks and a multitude of markings on top and underneath the leaves—in dark green, gray-green, purple or red.

No direct sunlight for this lovely, just lots of indirect light or carefully filtered sunlight. Keep the soil moist, and if possible, raise the humidity level to about 50 percent during the warm weather. For the brightest, showiest leaves, feed every other week with diluted, organic, water-soluble fertilizer. Night temperatures should be kept at about 65°F and daytime temperatures can go as high as 85°F. Make new plants by dividing old plant and roots each spring.

PEPEROMIA

You should try several of these because there are so many different varieties from which to choose. Native to tropical South America, this group of plants runs from tiny, flat-leaved varieties to variegated succulent-looking kinds. If you try no others, be sure to include at least Emerald Ripple, Watermelon and Blunt-leaved in your greenhouse.

foliage plants

CUT BACK TO ENCOURAGE FORM & FULLNESS. WANT TO SEE THE PLANT'S STRUCTURE? CUT OUT BRANCHES WHICH CROSS OR TOUCH. ALWAYS USE A CLEAN KNIFE OR SHEARS

Fortunately, the leaves and flowers are more attractive than the flower stalks, which tend to look like yellowish mouse tails.

Grow these in direct sunlight and watch your watering. They grow best when water is withheld until soil feels dry. Night temperatures around 65°F and day temperatures up around 85°F bring the best results. Dilute to one-half the amount of plant food recommended on bottle or package and use only three or four times a year. Use the leaves as stem cuttings to make as many new plants as you desire. Use the same soil mixture as for the rubber tree.

PHILODENDRON

At least 200 *Philodendron* species have come from South and Central America to grace our homes. There are so many different kinds of *Philodendron*, it is almost impossible not to find several you would like to grow. Pick from climbers and trailers, solid leaves and cut leaves, in greens that range from green greens to olives and all the way to almost-black greens. Best of all, these plants are practically impossible to kill.

Philodendron will do well when watered or left quite dry, when put in the sun or stuck in a dark corner. Try many varieties and, for best results, experiment to find how and where in your greenhouse they will do best. Start by giving filtered sunlight, just a bit of water (interestingly though, some can grow in water with no soil), and food three times a year. They like night temperatures in the 65°F range and day temperatures around 80°F.

The easiest way to make new plants is to use stem cuttings. Prune frequently to maintain an attractive shape and to prevent plant from getting scraggly looking. Like the rubber tree, if it grows too tall, remove the top and root it in water; once it's rooted, plant at the base of the parent plant.

PRAYER PLANT *(Maranta)*

The name is appropriate because *Maranta* truly do appear to "pray" each night. During the daylight hours the strikingly marked leaves remain in a horizontal position. At night they slowly rise to a vertical position which looks like hands raised in prayer. Found originally in Brazil, there are several fascinating varieties of prayer plants that are quite easy to grow in a greenhouse.

Keep in indirect sun and give the potting soil plenty of water, especially during warm weather. Feed every other month but stop feeding during late fall and winter months. Night temperatures of about 65°F and day temperatures of about 80°F are best. Divide roots to make new plants. For a special treat, move *Maranta* into your home and keep it under a lamp. You can "force" the plant to pray on order as you turn the light off and on.

SCHEFFLERA *(Brassaia)*

When buying schefflera, choose carefully. Usually long-lived, these pretty plants with their long leaves can also be very disappointing. When they are purchased in places other than garden shops and nurseries, they are frequently less than a good buy. Purchase your schefflera from a reputable dealer and be much more certain of getting a healthy plant. If careful about both choice and care, you could end up with a specimen that is easily as tall as you are.

Give these plants at least four hours of direct sunlight or bright light each day. They enjoy nighttime temperatures of about 65°F and daytime temperatures as high as 85°F. Water only when soil is quite dry. Feed with diluted liquid fertilizer every six months.

Keep plants within bounds by pruning off stem tips as soon as they reach desired height. Also prune suckers from the base. For new plants, seeds are your best bet.

foliage plants

DUNK A SMALL-LEAF PLANT TO WASH ITS LEAVES. COVER SOIL WITH FOIL OR PLASTIC BEFORE UP-ENDING

SNAKE PLANT *(Sansevieria)*

Here's another plant that is a survival expert. Natives of Africa, these plants, with their spear-like leaves will endure almost any treatment they get. The snake plant is a good gift for someone who usually has little success growing house plants.

But, for us . . . they will thrive with the proper care. There are two major varieties of *Sansevieria*, one short and one tall. The tall one, *Sansevieria trifasciata 'Laurentii,'* grows upright to about three feet tall if you let it, with wiggly bands of dark green on the yellow-edged spears. The short one, *'Hahnii,'* is squat and sort of bird's nest-like with the same dark-green-on-light-green markings, but not on the edges.

Grow snake plants in almost any kind of light but not direct sun. Water thoroughly and allow to dry out before watering again. These plants will *live* if watering is neglected, but will only *grow* if watered. Add fertilizer in May and August.

Temperatures of about 65°F at night and 80°F during the day suit them best. Offsets will come up near the main plant stem. Use them to make additional plants in general-purpose potting soil.

SWEDISH IVY *(Plectranthus)*

These are easy plants to grow, in addition to being lovely to look at. Almost anyone can have success raising either the standard types or the trailing varieties. Originally from Australia, Swedish ivy certainly seems misnamed, but is so-called because it was first grown as a house plant in Sweden. They come with different types of leaves: solid green, white edged or bronze-silver edged.

Grow in a general-purpose potting soil in bright light, but not direct sunlight. Try to keep soil slightly moist at all times. Feed about four times each year. Night temperatures of about 55°F and day temperatures about 20 degrees warmer bring out the best, most compact growth. Pinch extra-long stems as soon as they appear, to keep the plant from getting scraggly. Stick the pinchings directly into starting mix to get new plants. Cuttings root easily in water, too.

VELVET PLANT *(Gynura)*

You remember the old poetic joke, "I never saw a purple cow. . . ." Well, you don't see a purple plant too often either, and a hairy, purple plant at that. Natives of Java, these unusual plants have large leaves completely covered with short, brilliantly colored purple hair. When viewed in the right light, the plants cast an iridescent glow.

Velvet plant's most magnificent show will come when you place its foliage into sunlight for more than four hours each day. Feed with a dilute solution of liquid plant food once a month and water only enough to keep the soil just about moist. Night temperatures of about 65°F and day temperatures up to 85°F are just fine.

Pinch back the plant frequently to prevent it from becoming stringy and leggy and use the top cuttings to make new plants.

WANDERING JEW *(Zebrina, Cyanotis,* and *Tradescantia)*

That's right, it's called all of these names. Ask for *Zebrina pendula, Cyanotis vittata* or *Tradescantia tricolor* and you'll get a colorful creeper that trails, cascades and grows like crazy. Whichever you select and whichever color (green, silver, purple or white) appeals to you, put them into hanging baskets and watch them go.

Keep wandering Jew in bright, indirect light. Water when soil is just about dry and give a dilute fertilizer drink every other month. Night and day temperatures which suit you will suit the wandering Jew.

Snip off stems, stick back into pot and make a really full, cascading plant. When the plant is growing lushly, clip, clip, clip and give cuttings or newly started plants as gifts. They're easy to root in water.

special plants need special environments

Orchids and cacti. Quite a difference. From the sublime to the ridiculous? Beauty and the beast? Far from it. Both of these large plant families have great appeal for gardeners—frequently for widely divergent reasons. Cacti and orchids are poles apart in their greenhouse requirements, but both can be grown in almost any greenhouse (though not in the same greenhouse) if you give them special care, special attention and special considerations. One thing both have in common is you. Select either as your "hobby" plant and you have selected a hobby for a lifetime.

In talking about these two very different, yet very special, groups of plants, we find ourselves again ranting and enthusing over how wonderful they are and how you ought to try them. Perhaps we should apologize for driving you crazy with our "do this, try this, plant that" approach, but we can't. We drive ourselves crazy too. Each time we see something new, read about something new, try something new and discover something great, we want to share it with other gardeners. So there! So here! So share!

a whole world of orchids

Orchids are fascinating and frustrating. Some varieties can demand careful attention; others prefer to quietly do their own thing. They are tiny and huge, colorful and drab. They come from almost every part of the earth and combine horticultural mystery with a challenge for investigation by anyone who grows plants. All of this, plus the daredevil sagas of plant explorers risking their lives in search of rare species, makes orchid culture irresistible for greenhouse gardeners.

At one time, not too long ago, a rare clone commanded a "reasonable price" of up to $1500. However, research, experimentation and modern growing methods have put thousands of exotic orchids well within the reach of almost everyone. Common orchids can be obtained for as little as one dollar but, of course, you'll have to wait a while for them to bloom. Divisions of flowering-size orchids are generally available for under $10, while similar divisions of award-winning clones cost about $20.

Be warned about *orchiditis.* This not-so-rare disease among gardeners first shows up as a passing interest in these marvelous plants. It proceeds to a desire to grow them and then increases very rapidly until you must grow more and more of them. In its critical stage, *orchiditis* affects your brain, causing you to feel you never have enough orchids and never have enough room to properly house your collection. You will begin to feel as if you are losing a child each time you must part with even a single specimen.

If you are not afraid of contracting this disease and want to take your chances with the age-old fascination of orchids, the following are some of the easier-grown genera with which you may begin a challenging, lifelong hobby. We've started with one of the easiest, *Brassavola,* as a prototype to illustrate how simple orchid culture can really be. On the other genera, we tell only how their care differs from that of the *Brassavola.* At the end of this section you will find some general guidelines for the culture of all orchids.

special plants

BRASSAVOLA

These come from tropical America and bring with them wonderful white, yellow and very pale-green flowers. These orchids are especially suitable for a greenhouse as they rarely grow taller than a foot and yet, every inch is packed with incredibly fragrant (some are night fragrant), very long-lasting, large blossoms.

Grow *Brassavola* in a mixture of chopped bark, shredded tree-fern fiber or redwood bark pieces and perlite, not in soil. Another good way to grow them is attached to a slab of bark or wood. Keep them in bright, indirect sunlight for as many hours as possible. If sunlight is short in your area, plan on installing fluorescents to grow these orchids. These plants do well at daytime temperatures around 70°F and night-time temperatures about 10 degrees lower.

Place the potted plant on pebbles in a tray of water, but do not allow water to come above the level of the pebbles. Humidity is the name of the game when growing orchids, but ventilation is important too. Orchids demand clean, well-circulated air. Small electric fans will help circulate air in your greenhouse and keep your orchids happy and healthy. When watering, water thoroughly, then allow potting mixture to become reasonably dry before you water again. Feed once each month with a diluted water-soluble fertilizer, high in nitrogen.

BRASSIA

These evergreens from tropical Africa are called spider orchids because their flowers look spidery (now that's a welcome bit of logic in an otherwise crazy world). Plants grow easily to about 15 inches high and produce white to yellow flowers with brown spots. You can also find many other color, spot and size variations in this genus. These plants like sun and warmth. Grow in temperatures of at least 75°F during the day and 10 degrees cooler at night, and supply a minimum of four hours of strong, direct sunlight each day. Other growing requirements are the same as *Brassavola*, except that for these plants the potting mix should be kept moist at all times instead of allowing it to dry out a bit between waterings. Also, they are sensitive to stale potting mixture, so repot yearly.

CATTLEYA

These are probably best known for their appearance by the thousands in the annual Rose Bowl Parade each New Year's Day. They are also the orchids that are usually made into corsages. Very easy to grow as greenhouse plants, *Cattleya* produce large, showy flowers in white, mauve, pink, lavender and other assorted shades. Give them at least four hours of sun each day, but do keep them out of extreme heat. Too much heat will quickly ruin them. Push the humidity up to 50 to 70 percent and keep daytime temperatures around 70°F and nighttime around 60°F. Always water thoroughly, then allow potting mix to get quite dry between waterings. Other requirements same as for *Brassavola.*

CYMBIDIUM

Great masses of full-sized flowers on miniature-sized plants make these orchids perfect for greenhouse growing. Colors include white, pink, bronze, deep red, green, yellow and shades in between. Keep in at least four hours of sunlight each day, but avoid high-noon heat or leaves will brown. Daytime temperatures around 70°F and nighttime of 50° to 55°F are ideal. Keep the potting mix wet. Repot only when absolutely necessary, if you want to keep this plant blooming most profusely. Other requirements same as for *Brassavola.*

DENDROBIUM

Most of these orchids come from Australia and New Guinea where there are both evergreen and deciduous types. There are hundreds of different species within this popular genus. All like a superabundance of indirect sunlight each day. Keep daylight temperatures around 60° to 65°F and nighttime temperatures no lower than 55°F. When plants are

special plants

growing, keep potting mix well moistened and feed monthly with high-nitrogen fertilizer. During late fall and winter stop feeding and only supply enough water so plant doesn't shrivel. These, like cymbidiums, do not like repotting. Only do it when absolutely necessary. Other requirements same as for *Brassavola*.

EPIDENDRUM

These native Americans are of the spray-flower type. Many produce flowers all year long in great profusion. For them to produce flowers in abundance, they'll need plenty of sunlight and misting, as well as water. Just to remind you, there must be good aeration of the soil mixture, and a drying out between waterings. Keep daytime temperatures in the 70°F range and nighttime temperature about 55°F. Other requirements same as for *Brassavola*.

LAELIA

Within this genus are some of the best orchids for your greenhouse. Some blooms are as large, colorful and abundant as *Cattleyas*, which is often bred with *Laelia* to form *Laeliacattleya* hybrids, the most colorful orchids suitable for growing indoors. Give at least four hours of sunlight each day. Watch drainage carefully. Water only when potting mix feels dry. Maintain daytime temperatures of about 70°F and nighttime temperatures about 70°F. Other requirements same as for *Brassavola*.

There are many more orchid genera from which you can choose once you've caught *orchiditis*. And then, of course there are the hybrids. *Odontoglossum*, an Andes beauty with flower spikes that grow to three feet, is often bred with other genera to produce dramatic hybrids, many of which can be grown in your greenhouse and under lights. You will have to do some experimenting with them, because the different kinds have widely differing requirements, but they are well worth the time and effort. Having been enchanted by all their flowering beauty, you'll agree.

Once you start growing orchids, it doesn't really matter which varieties you choose. You'll never get them out of your mind or heart. Investigate the vast genera of orchids available for greenhouse growth. Some are more difficult to grow than others, but you'll find them all fascinating, exquisite and satisfying. The following are some general suggestions, valid and valuable for all orchid growing, that will help you get started. Once your first experimental plants are doing well, you'll have the basic knowledge as well as the courage and interest to start experimenting on your own. You'll soon develop ways to help your orchids do their best in the specific atmosphere of your greenhouse.

• Choose intelligently. Start out with plants that will stand the best chance of success in your greenhouse. If you select kinds that are successfully grown only by commercial greenhouse professionals, you will expend much time and effort to prove that they are successfully grown only by commercial greenhouse professionals. Take your time. Start out easy. You'll get to the tough ones—when you are also tough enough to handle them. Start slow, experiment steadily and, like the tortoise, you'll get to your goal long before the reckless speed demon.

• Keep away from complicated, special soil mixes. Make your own, with no soil, but two parts ground fir-tree bark, one part redwood bark pieces and one part perlite. Barks are deficient in nitrogen so you will have to compensate. Also, they break down, becoming a kind of mud, which means you have to repot, and this may slow the plant's growth. Osmunda fiber is also good, but it takes getting used to for good results and is more expensive. Always put your potting mix into a pot with a large drainage hole in the bottom. (Remember to crock it, of course.) Drainage is critical with many orchids and though the proper potting mix helps, you will defeat yourself if there is no drainage hole. Two or more holes are even better.

• Orchids also need lots of air. That's where the drainage hole plays a dual role. It not only allows excess water out of the pot, it allows air to get in to the roots. If your plant sits in water, with the roots covered with water, it will not be long before the roots rot and the plant dies.

special plants

- Although watering requirements differ for just about each species, one thing is certain for all; orchids dislike overwatering. For most orchids, soak once or twice a week, depending on the humidity condition in your greenhouse. Wait until the potting mix dries out a bit before you water again.
- Fertilize your plants about once every three weeks with a carefully measured, light dose of high-nitrogen fertilizer, like 30-10-10, to promote substantial healthy growth. Your best bet is a liquid fertilizer, diluted considerably. Never, never toss in a little extra for "good measure." Follow the instructions exactly as they are written on the container. This is definitely neither the place nor the plant with which to ad lib.
- Watch temperatures carefully. There must be about a 15-degree drop between day and night temperatures, or no blooms. Without this drop you may get many leaves but you certainly won't get many, if any, flowers.
- Give your orchids plenty of sun, but screen them from the hot midday blast. During the spring and summer, providing sun is no problem. However, late in the year you may have to supplement your sunlight with fluorescent lights. Time the hours that strong sunlight reaches your orchids. They need a total of 13 to 16 hours of light a day. If there are not enough, give the extra light needed, artificially.
- Orchids thrive where there is ventilation and die where there is none. Best growth will be found when fresh air circulates around the plants and, as we said, around the roots. The humidity level in your greenhouse will need to be high to grow orchids. If there is little ventilation (air circulation), this high humidity will cause rotting and that you don't need.
- Finally, maintain a humidity level in your greenhouse of at least 50 to 60 percent. You should have a hygrometer to measure this. If the humidity drops, misting is in order. To keep your greenhouse humid you can install a soaker hose on the ceiling, set out barrels or pails full of water and water your paths and paved areas often.

desert cacti and other succulents

Leave the high humidity world of orchids and move to an entirely different world. A world of dryness, of plants without leaves, of beauty that is frequently in the eye of the beholder. Start thinking about the world of cacti and other succulents.

Chin, bunny ears, rat-tail, sheep wool, beaver's tail, goat's horn, powder puff. Spare parts for a toy stuffed-animal manufacturer? Not quite. Try these. Turk's cap, Joseph's coat, Irish mitt, bishop's hood, devil's pincushion. Biblical and ethnic terms? Would you believe they are all cacti? Just some of the more than 1300 different species. With names like these no wonder so many people are becoming more and more enthused about growing cacti. If you're still not intrigued, how about names like seven sisters, old man, old lady, golden stars, organ pipe and sea urchin?

Cacti are surrounded by so many myths and misconceptions, it's no wonder many gardeners are afraid to try them. Before going any further, a few important facts. All cacti are succulents, but not all succulents are cacti. Got that? Let's go on. Succulent, in the plant world, means just what it means in the other world, juicy. Succulent plants usually have fleshy leaves, stems or both. Cacti are just one part of the succulent group and are, almost without exception, plants without leaves. Their bodies are ribbed or flattened and are able to

special plants

store quantities of water. They are easily recognizable because of their distinctive stem shape which can be round, columnar, jointed, fluted, angular or notched. And when they flower, their blooms are magnificent and awesome.

A prevalent misconception is that cacti live and grow in pure sand, require no water and thrive in beastly hot sun. They are really much more like "regular" plants than most people realize. They definitely need food, water and light to grow, and prefer something a little more substantial than pure sand as the place to set down their roots.

Though cactus plants are now available just about everywhere, including your local supermarket, buy them from either a reliable local nursery or mail-order supplier. Though supermarkets and dime stores often offer bargains, keep the survival percentage on your side—buy from a reputable grower. Start out conservatively with a few small plants. Don't worry if, when you buy them, they seem too large for their pots; they like it that way.

Select plants that are sturdy, uniformly colored, nicely balanced in shape, have no scars, bangs or nicks and are not in the least shriveled. When you get them home, don't rush them to the hottest, sunniest part of the greenhouse. Allow them to become acclimated to their new environment. Keep them in an indirectly lighted area for the first few days and then move them to their permanent home.

In addition, after bringing your new cacti home, check the pots. If they came in plastic pots or in pots without large drainage holes, repot them as soon as possible. The best containers for cacti are unglazed clay pots with large drainage holes in the bottom. Keeping these plants in plastic or glazed pots that retain moisture will increase tremendously the risk that you'll lose your plants through root rot.

Here's a rule of thumb for proper pot selection: For vertical growing plants use a pot with a diameter half the height of the plant, one that is deeper than it is wide. For rounded cacti and other succulents, use a pot that is two inches larger in diameter than the plant. It is also important that you use either a brand new pot or one that has been thoroughly scrubbed with hot, soapy water then carefully rinsed to foil fungus spores which lurk in dirty pots.

Growing cacti and other succulents in your greenhouse is a unique experience. You must pay extra-special attention to the amounts of light and water you make available to your plants.

There are so many different kinds of cacti and other succulents available, it is almost impossible to choose. Perhaps your best bet is to start out with some "sure-thing" cacti for purple thumbs and expand from there. Here are a few wonderful varieties of desert cacti that would make an excellent starting collection.

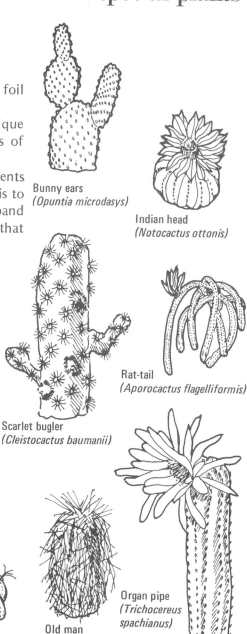

Bunny ears
(*Opuntia microdasys*)

Indian head
(*Notocactus ottonis*)

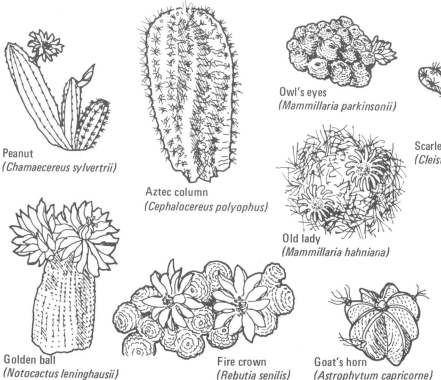

Peanut
(*Chamaecereus sylvertrii*)

Aztec column
(*Cephalocereus polyophus*)

Owl's eyes
(*Mammillaria parkinsonii*)

Old lady
(*Mammillaria hahniana*)

Scarlet bugler
(*Cleistocactus baumanii*)

Rat-tail
(*Aporocactus flagelliformis*)

Golden ball
(*Notocactus leninghausii*)

Fire crown
(*Rebutia senilis*)

Goat's horn
(*Astrophytum capricorne*)

Old man
(*Cephalocereus senilis*)

Organ pipe
(*Trichocereus spachianus*)

special plants

LIGHT

When buying these plants, choose only those whose light requirements you can provide. Don't make it a "maybe it'll work" situation. Either you have enough light or you don't. Either you can grow them and they'll do well or you can't. If you decide to tackle cacti, it may be necessary to supplement your light source with fluorescent or special incandescent bulbs. Desert cacti need as much bright light as possible. Keep them in the sunniest, the southernmost part of your greenhouse. If they don't get enough sun they'll grow too fast reaching for light and will lose their wonderful characteristic shape. Also, remember that cacti must have sun if they are to produce flowers.

WATER

All succulents need to be watered far less often than plants that do not store water. Be careful of overwatering, which leads to rotting of roots and stems. Except in the growing season, watering once a month is often sufficient. Soil must be thoroughly dry quite far down before you water again.

SOIL MIX

The soil for succulents should be porous, so that water drains through rapidly. A suitable mix for clay pots is one part sandy loam or garden soil, one part leaf mold and two parts coarse, washed builders' sand or perlite. This is only one of an almost endless list of recipes for soil (or soilless) mixes. Whichever one you choose, remember that succulents need nourishment and an open mix to permit rapid drainage of water and free entry of oxygen to the roots.

POTTING

Place a pebble or pot shard over the drainage hole, then add a layer of gravel. Partly fill the pot with soil mix, center your plant and place it to accommodate the roots. Fill the pot with soil, constantly tapping it to settle the soil. The pot is full when the soil level is about one-half inch below the rim of the pot. Do not plant too deeply. If part of the body of the plant is buried it will rot. A layer of gravel on top adds neatness and attractiveness; it also serves to keep the sensitive base of the plant dry. After potting, do not water for one week to allow for healing of any damaged roots.

SEASONAL CARE

Cacti and other succulents grow in the warm months of the year and will need to be watered as often as the soil dries out. The more sun the plants get, the more frequent watering they need. Begin with a single watering in March and add extra water more often as needed (depending on weather conditions) through August. When the plants begin active growth, feed them every four weeks with a balanced fertilizer (15-30-15), diluted to one-third the recommended strength (one teaspoon per gallon of water instead of one tablespoon). Most succulents are slow growers and should not be forced with too much feeding. Stop all feeding in July.

In early September prepare the plants for dormancy by lengthening the intervals between waterings. With mature cacti a winter resting period is necessary, that is, little or no water from November to March. Do not force your cacti into growth by watering them in winter. With little sun and regular watering, they will become weak and spindly. A dry, cool (45° to 50°F) winter resting place is the best insurance for flowers in spring and summer.

All succulents need fresh air and they will welcome and respond to a "summer vacation" outdoors if suitable space is available. Bring them back into your greenhouse or into your house in the fall.

WASH AN OLD MAN CACTUS IN SOAPY WATER, RINSE & BLOW DRY

WHEN REPOTTING A CACTUS USE GLOVES & A RAG SLING

try it
-you'll like it

In this chapter we'll suggest and describe different projects we think are fun to learn about and do. They will be as varied as you can possibly imagine (or maybe even more so) and should lead you into more and more fun in your greenhouse. You will find a greenhouse gives you the room to "fool around" and try many projects you didn't have space for before. After all, how many windowsills, table tops or kitchen counters can you appropriate?

PLANTS FROM PITS, SEEDS AND NUTS

Much of the fun in gardening comes from getting something for nothing. You can grow beautiful plants by utilizing pits, seeds, acorns and nuts, all of which are lying on the ground or heading for the garbage pail. Success is almost always assured and the variety of plants you can grow this way is almost endless.

Avocado

We'll start with that most famous (or should that be infamous?) of all indoor plants, started from one whopper of a seed, the avocado. We don't even like avocados but keep buying them, just for the pits. (At least we save money by buying them when they are past their prime.)

Remove the pulp from the pit and wash the pit thoroughly in warm water. Remove the brown skin. If it doesn't come off easily, let the pit stand in warm water overnight and peel it off the next day. The pit will then be clean and smooth.

Push three toothpicks into the pit, evenly spaced about three-quarters of an inch up from the bottom (flat end). Place the pit, with the toothpicks resting on the rim, into a small jar or glass. Fill the container with warm water so the bottom half of the pit is submerged. Set the glass aside in a warm spot out of direct sun.

CERAMIC AVOCADO STARTER

Check daily to make sure the water is always covering the pit bottom. Keep watching for signs of growth and don't despair. It may seem to take forever, and it can take weeks or even months. The pit will eventually crack, roots will show and a shoot will head up. As long as the water remains clear, all's well. If the water should cloud or begin to smell, throw everything out, buy another avocado and start over.

When the sprout is eight inches tall, remove the top four inches. Two weeks after that it's time to pot the plant. Select a good-sized pot. Fill it one-fourth full with a mixture of two parts potting soil and one part coarse builders' sand. Remove toothpicks and place pit in pot, gently spreading roots. Slowly add more soil mixture until all but the top half of the seed is covered. Carefully add water to the soil until it is damp and settled. Add more soil until it is once again level with the halfway mark of the pit. Place a support in the pot now. Your avocado will need support eventually and placing it now will avoid tearing roots as you ram it in later. Place the pot in the sun and keep the soil moist at all times. Feed immediately after potting and every two months thereafter. Encourage branching by pinching the bud off the center stalk of the plant.

try it

HUMIDITY LEVEL IS RAISED WHEN POTS ARE SET ON A PEBBLE TRAY WITH WATER IN THE BOTTOM (DON'T LET POTS SIT IN WATER)

Citrus Plants

Citrus seeds, normally discarded, are free and fun to grow. Oranges, lemons, limes, tangerines and others can be grown easily and quickly. Plant three or four seeds about one-half inch deep in potting soil. Use pots, margarine containers, poly cups or whatever. Water the soil and place in a dark spot until seeds germinate. Then move seedlings into the sun until they reach about five inches. Transplant the five-inch seedlings into individual pots containing one part good topsoil, one part sand and one part peat moss.

Citrus trees like temperatures of about 55°F, light in the winter and sunlight in the summer. Fertilize once a month. Once each year transplant to the next larger clay pot. These plants are lovely, with very attractive, dark-green, glossy leaves. Flowers and sometimes fruit are possible in several years.

Oaks

To prove that mighty oaks do indeed from little acorns grow, go gather up some acorns. Set them in your refrigerator for about two months; then remove the little "hat" from the acorn and set the acorn, point down, into the mouth of a soft-drink bottle, filled with water so the bottom is always wet. In two or three weeks the acorn will sprout and roots will grow down into the bottle. When the roots are several inches long, pot in a mixture of good topsoil or potting mixture. Place the pot in the sun and water when dry (not *dry* but dry). Acorns can also be planted directly in soil. The oak will grow to about four or five feet in the greenhouse; then it should be transferred outdoors.

FORCING BULBS

If you, like us, get misty eyed when you see the first crocus or discover a tulip's tiny leaf tip suddenly appear one day, you'll get the same delight from forcing bulbs. And, if you've never tried it, or thought *you* couldn't do it, try it now. There is no magic or mystery in the process.

The term "forcing" is actually a bit misleading. It actually means "shortening" the length of time it takes a bulb to root, mature and then bloom. We can't make the bulb do anything until the time and conditions are right; we just hurry things along a bit.

We'll deal with hardy bulbs, so-called because they are hardy enough to get started under rather cold conditions—temperatures of 45°F or even lower. If your greenhouse is kept at much higher temperatures than this, try a more tender bulb.

Narcissus (also known as daffodils or jonquils) are the easiest to force of the hardy bulbs. Also, almost guaranteed for good results are hyacinths, iris, crocus, tulips and amaryllis. We've listed the easiest first, the most difficult last, so if you are new at this game, try them in the order listed to avoid aggravation.

Always buy the biggest and best bulbs you can afford; this is no place to look for bargains. Make sure they are plump and blemish-free.

Hardy bulbs require certain conditions to be induced to flower indoors. First, they'll need a two- to three-month rooting period in a very cool (40° to 45°F) place. During this time they should be kept covered (or in the dark).

Their next growth period should be in temperatures of up to 50° to 55°F (that of most greenhouses) with a little light. Under a bench is perfect. This period lasts from two to three weeks. After this they are moved up onto a bench to soak up as much sun and light as they possibly can. They stay there until you see the buds forming. At this point bring them into the house. Temperatures in the house are probably a little below 70°F, which allows them to keep their flowers for the longest possible period. Keeping them out of direct sun while blooming is also suggested. Also, contrary to what you may have heard, bulbs which have been forced *can* be planted outdoors and after a year or two of rest will bloom again with no special attention.

try it

FERNS

Here's something for every greenhouse: Plants that date back over 400 million years and lived when the dinosaurs roamed. Ferns may be filmy, wispy or leathery, but are always easy to grow in a greenhouse.

Their native environment is one in which there is little sun, lots of humidity and loamy, spongy soil like that under the trees in a forest. When the time comes for you to plant, make sure your planting soil combines peat moss, sand, rotted leaves, humus, well-rotted manure and well-decayed compost. Good drainage is vital. A fern's need for high humidity and little light makes shady parts of each greenhouse the perfect environment. Ferns like moist soil, but be careful not to overwater; a good balance is necessary. These plants should never stand in water or dry out completely.

Read through the following descriptions and choose the varieties which appeal to you. Some have flowers, some berries, some are lacy, some are not. The choice is up to you.

Asparagus fern *(Asparagus plumosus)*, popular in bouquets, enjoys temperatures of 50° to 55°F. It is, however, erroneously called a fern because of its minutely divided leaves which resemble fern fronds. *Asparagus sprengeri*, a relative, has tiny white flowers which are replaced by red berries.

Bird's nest fern *(Asplenium nidus)* likes 50° to 55°F temperatures also. It grows into a shape that resembles a bird's nest.

Leather fern *(Polystichum adiantiforme)* has the same temperature requirements as the asparagus and bird's nest. The fronds are actually thick and leathery but appear wispy.

The maidenhair fern *(Adiantum tenerum)* is a compact grower. It definitely doesn't like sun and prefers slightly higher temperatures, 60° to 65°F, than the ferns already discussed. High humidity and lots of water will keep it happy.

Mother fern *(Asplenium bulbiferum)* is another one that likes the 50° to 55°F range. Its dark green, curving fronds are beautiful in hanging baskets.

When purchasing ferns, ask the nurseryperson if they are the rhizomatous or non-rhizomatous kind. Rhizomatous ones, like the leather fern and maidenhair fern, are "covered" rather than planted. Smooth the area where they'll go and lay the rhizomes in place. Using the same soil mixture as described earlier, barely cover the rhizome and its roots. If necessary, place a few stones on top of the rhizome to keep it in place until the roots take hold.

Non-rhizomatous ferns should be planted so their crowns are just level with the soil. When planting, watch to be sure that the old soil mark is visible.

Ferns are very attractive when placed in hanging baskets and may be alternated between your home and greenhouse where they, and you, may enjoy the best of both worlds.

With proper watering, fertilizing and not much sun, ferns will multiply beautifully, give you much pleasure and last for years and years.

JUNGLE CACTI

Earlier we talked about desert cacti. There is a completely different world of jungle or epiphytic cacti, including the popular Christmas cactus, with completely different growing requirements. These epiphytes grow, not in an arid desert area, but in a tropical rain forest at an elevation of about 2,000 to 4,000 feet. They cling to the trunks and branches of trees, their roots sticking out into the air. They neither look nor act anything at all like the cacti we know from the southwestern United States.

To grow jungle cacti in a greenhouse you must approximate, as closely as possible, the conditions under which they grew in nature. No cactus collection is complete without the wonderfully spectacular house plant, Christmas cactus *(Schlumbergera bridgesii)*. Another good variety for greenhouses is the Thanksgiving cactus *(Zygocactus truncatus)*. The following suggestions are designed to get you magnificent flowers during the holiday season and once again in the spring.

Use a clay pot with lots of drainage material in the bottom. Plant in rich, porous soil made up of leaf mold or humusy loam with sharp sand, grit or small pebbles to make a loose mixture. Water regularly so plants never dry out. Young plants in small containers must be carefully watched, for they will dry out more quickly.

Jungle cacti like a moderately cool environment. Keep in direct sunlight in winter when the sun is weak; east or west exposure is good. In spring, summer and early fall move plants out of direct midday sun. Instead, give them filtered sunlight or early morning or late afternoon sun. Put your plant outdoors in summer, if possible, in an airy, partially shaded place. Feed with a high-nitrogen fertilizer a few times during the late spring and early summer when new stem segments are forming.

In early September bring your jungle cacti into your greenhouse, choosing a cool spot where they can rest. The critical period in bud development lasts for eight weeks, approximately September 15 through November 15. During these weeks, keep your plant on the dry side, watering only once a week or less. Also in this period, do not move the plant to another location or change its position until buds are half formed, or they will drop. Electric lights prevent bud formation, too. If working in your greenhouse at night during the autumn months, cover your jungle cacti with a dark cloth. Feed with low-nitrogen, high-phosphate fertilizer several times during September and October.

INSECT-EATING PLANTS

Carnivorous plants will amuse and fascinate almost everyone. They are plants which "eat" insects and are true showoffs to boot, gladly putting on their act at the drop of a bug (or even a bit of raw hamburger if bug catching doesn't interest you). The greenhouse is the perfect place for this type of plant because it loves moisture and humidity.

Of course the plants don't actually "eat" the insect. They trap it, using slightly varying methods, and digest the totally helpless creature.

Everyone's favorite and the best example of a carnivorous plant is the Venus's-flytrap. It is so readily available with full description and instructions we'll ignore it and move along to some others.

Butterwort *(Pinguicula)*

The leaves of this plant are coated with a sticky, gummy substance. When an unwary insect lands, it's like landing on flypaper and just as effective. The insect's stuck in more ways than one. The leaf then curls around it providing a "digesting container" and that's it for that bug.

Pitcher Plant *(Sarracenia)*

These plants have pitcher-shaped flowers ("the better to catch bugs my dears") which hold liquid. The liquid lures the insect to enter the flower where it is trapped. The lining of the flower is composed of downward pointed hairs which prevent an upward climb. Once trapped, the insect drowns in the liquid and is digested by the juices.

Sundew *(Drosera)*

This plant is the sneakiest of all. On its leaves are tentacle-like hairs coated with a smelly sticky liquid which lures insects to it. Once caught, that's it. Stuck but good. The hairs then turn inward pressing the insect into the juices which digest it.

Culture

Naturally, in a greenhouse situation there will be few insects available for the plants to trap themselves. It will be up to you to "feed" the plant. Don't feed it too often and never use fertilizer. These plants' roots and leaves neither need nor want fertilizer and by being too good to them you might kill the plant. Carnivorous plants have no other special requirements. They do well in average soil, light and water.

An interesting fact that sometimes surprises people is that these three carnivorous varieties are native to the continental United States and are a tiny percentage of the hundreds of varieties to be found around the world.

try it

PERFORMING PLANTS

Here are some fascinating plants that will keep you and your family entertained, amused and amazed. You will gaze in wonder each time they perform. All may be grown from seed, and all will do well in the house also.

Animated Oats *(Avena sterilis)*

The name alone is enough to attract attention. But animated it is, doing a twisting and turning act every time a source of water is placed near it. This plant can be started from seed and, once sprouted, should be thinned to about six inches apart. It likes the sun and grows to a mature height of about three feet. It can move outdoors with success and can also be dried for flower arrangements.

Artillery Plant *(Pilea microphylla)*

The maturing flower buds literally explode when they open. The violent popping flings pollen all over the place. Should several open at the same time, you can imagine the effect. Keep their soil moist and in full sun. An added bonus is that they can be propagated from cuttings.

ANIMATED OATS

ARTILLERY PLANT

Gas Plant *(Dictamnus albus)*

This plant is also called burning bush because it gives off a gas that catches fire, for a split second, when a lighted match is held near it. If seeds are sown in the greenhouse in the fall, they will be ready for transplanting outdoors the following spring. By midsummer they'll be ready, on a still, quiet night to perform their magic act.

GAS
PLANT

Prayer Plant *(Maranta leuconeura kerchoveana)*

This plant is especially interesting to have because it performs every single night. It moves its leaves slowly but visibly upward, so they are ultimately all facing the sky. You can actually see them move if you'll take the time to sit and watch. By morning they have returned to their normal, flattened position. Pot in rich soil, keep moist and give lots of light or sun. Divide clumps for sharing.

Telegraph Plant *(Desmodium motorium)*

This plant nods up and down in rhythm, giving the appearance of a telegraph key tapping out a message, or a semaphore signaling. Or maybe it just nods its head when the conversation gets dull. Whatever its reasons, it's incredible to watch the rhythmic motion. An Indian native, it loves living in the warm and humid atmosphere of the greenhouse and can also move outdoors.

PRAYER
PLANT

TELEGRAPH
PLANT

FRUIT TREES

Perhaps one of the things that most excites and delights an Easterner, visiting in California or Florida, is the sight of a real orange tree, growing in someone's backyard. Now that you have a greenhouse, you too can have your own orange tree, as well as lemon, lime or even kumquat, no matter where you make your home.

Lemon Trees

Of all the indoor citrus plants, probably the most exciting is the Ponderosa lemon *(Citrus limonia 'Ponderosa')*. Even when kept at a carefully pruned height of four feet, the tree continues to bear its spectacular fruit, each one weighing up to three pounds. The tree must be propped as soon as fruit appears because the lemons become heavier throughout the five to six months it takes for each fruit to mature.

The Meyer lemon *(Citrus limonia 'Meyeri')* also grows well indoors and produces average-sized fruit. Even pruned to a height of two feet, it will produce well. Both the Ponderosa and Meyer varieties have beautiful, shiny green leaves and pointy spines. When the Meyer flowers, there is a bonus of sweet scent and attractive, waxy, white flowers.

Lime Trees

Here comes a shock. Sit down for this one: Did you know limes are actually yellow when they are fully ripe? The low-growing *Citrus aurantofolia* is an outstanding and attractive selection for the greenhouse. Wait for the fruit to turn yellow. You'll be surprised and delighted, because the taste of the fully ripened lime is far sweeter than it is when eaten green.

Mandarin Orange Trees

For small, indoor orange trees, you can grow and enjoy either Calamondin *(Citrus mitis)* or Otaheite *(Citrus taitensis)*. The disadvantage here is that neither tree bears fruit that you would enjoy eating. However, it is delicious made into orange marmalade. The trees are low growing and usually remain about two feet tall. They are attractive in appearance as are their flowers and fruit. Another bonus? The flowers have a wonderful aroma. Remember orange blossoms?

An amazing thing about the fruit of these trees is that it can remain on the tree for almost two years. What a conversation piece! Bring the tree into the house when you expect guests and it will bask in the spotlight for the evening—or even several months.

Kumquat Trees

A fun thing to grow (especially if you have paid the price for a small box in the supermarket) is the kumquat. Choose between the dwarf *Fortunella hindisi,* which never grows over 12 inches indoors, and *Fortunella margarita,* which grows to two feet tall. Kumquats are eaten skin and all, and the delicate flavor of the home-grown fruit is superb.

Culture

In the winter, citrus trees like indirect light but not sun. Night temperatures of 50° to 55°F and day temperatures no higher than 70°F are ideal. Plan on watering once a week, and when you water, water well. Give them a good chance to drink all they want. When your tree has absorbed all it wants, drain off the excess from its saucer or tray. Wait until the soil at the top of the pot becomes *almost* dry before watering again. Don't allow the soil to dry out completely. Once that happens it's too late. The plant starts to lose its leaves and slowly begins to die. Don't get hung up on that "once-a-week" phrase; watch and water when necessary.

Don't concern yourself too much with pruning; these trees rarely need any. An occasional go round to maintain a pretty shape or trim out a dead limb is all there should be.

Once again, as you did with your greenhouse-grown tomatoes and some other vegetables, get in on Mother Nature's act. Pollination by hand will assure you of a fine citrus crop. Follow the same suggestions given for vegetables on page 81.

try it

HYDROPONICS

Hydroponics, also called water culture, soilless culture or nutrient-solution culture, simply means growing plants in water instead of soil. Although it has become more popular in recent years, it certainly is not a new idea, having started in England in 1699.

When gardening hydroponically, you must follow the rules. Your plants will require light, water, temperature levels of 60° to 80°F during the day and 60°F at night (for warm-weather crops) and about 10 degrees cooler day and night for cool-season crops. They also need oxygen, carbon dioxide and 13 other minerals and elements.

Start small, using a quart jar for your first experiment. Cover the jar so it is lightproof. Fill the jar with water to which you have added liquid fertilizer, using one-fourth the amount recommended on the bottle for the same amount of liquid. Be sure to leave an inch of air space. Find a cork, stopper or something that will plug up the mouth of the jar. Cut a hole in it just large enough to slip the plant through, yet snug enough to support the plant. Be sure the roots extend down far enough to enter the solution.

For larger experiments, use your own imagination and produce whatever designs you can. Aquariums, window boxes, rectangular waterproof planters or whatever you can find are fine. Plants may be supported from the top by pulling them through holes in plywood, mesh or even cork board. Just be sure the top is not sealed, excluding air from the solution and roots.

Hydroponic gardens must be watched every day to make sure the level of solution has remained relatively constant. In warm and hot weather, it will be necessary to add solution every day to keep the volume steady. Every two to three weeks empty all the solution and replace with a new mixture.

Since, among other things, hydroponic gardening has been talked about as being a possible solution to the world food crisis caused by increasing loss of usable farm land, perhaps it is a good idea to try it. An interesting experiment might be to grow your Patio tomatoes hydroponically. Try one plant grown in water and one in soil. Compare them for taste and quality and then decide whether hydroponic gardening is the answer.

You can try almost any plant in your hydroponic gardens. Both flowering plants and foliage plants will grow in water. Try Chinese evergreen, *Maranta*, *Impatiens* or wandering Jew.

BROMELIADS

It is rare that we go into our local nursery that they don't have 10 or 12 perfect and perfectly exquisite bromeliads on display. Not only is the foliage at its peak of perfection but there, right in the center, is one magnificent flower. Bromeliads are so unusual in appearance and so lovely it would be a pity to have a greenhouse and not enjoy what they have to offer.

Bromeliads and pineapples are of the same family, and when you think about the way a pineapple top looks it makes sense. Bromeliads are quite unusual because they are among the very few plants that are able to take all their nourishment from the air, not from the soil. (They need no fertilizer.) You can put them in the craziest places and they will not only grow but thrive—in pots, from greenhouse supports, on trees (small ones in the greenhouse) or in hanging baskets.

Bromeliads love light (but not strong sunlight), yet will also do very well in shade. Their favorite growing temperature is 65°F.

The soil should be a mixture of equal parts coarse sand and peat moss. Water well and keep the soil moist because this plant loves a moist atmosphere. Allow it to dry out occasionally to be sure that rot does not occur. Also keep the little cuplike area at the base of the leaves filled with water.

You can root a pineapple top and start your own. Just cut off the top of a fresh pineapple so it has about two inches of fruit. Let the leaf part dry for two days. Place the flat side down in sand, water or peat moss. It won't be long before you have a new pineapple plant, *Ananas*.

Other bromeliad possibilities include: *Aechmea, Billbergia, Cryptan-*

thus, Guzmania, Neoregelia, Tillandsia and *Vriesea.* The leaves range in color from green to yellow striped with dark red, to green with yellow speckles. The flowers, as lovely as they are, sometimes take second place to the beautiful leaves. Flowers of red, white or yellow appear and make these plants worthy of even more of your time and interest.

AFRICAN VIOLETS

A long time ago, when we first started growing house plants, African violets were the worst and most consistent disasters. We just could not get them to grow. Disgusted by our lack of success we finally did some extra homework, read the rules and followed them. Result: gorgeous, prolific and long-lasting African violets of every size, color and description. So, now you too know the secret: There is no mystery. Just give African violets what they want and you can't fail.

There are many wonderful qualities in African violets that make them almost perfect for greenhouse growing. They are not too large, they flower freely through the entire year, they are easy to propagate, come in a tremendous range of colors and leaf shapes and are absolutely gorgeous when in bloom. Here are some not-so-secret ingredients required for success.

Light

African violets, contrary to popular misconception, enjoy and need plenty of light. Not the direct, intense sunlight of summer, but indirect or curtain-shaded light. Meager winter light should be supplemented with artificial light for several hours each day.

Water

Another common error is thinking that because these flowers are native to a hot, tropical climate, they should be kept moist at all times. Not so. Overwatering is a good way to kill them off. Don't water until the soil is slightly dry to the touch—not hard, caked and *dry*, but slightly dry. You may water from the top or bottom, whichever you prefer. If watering from the top, water until it runs out the bottom. Then, whichever way you've gotten that saucer full, let it sit that way for about a half hour. After that time, drain off whatever water has not been absorbed.

Food

African violets are nibblers. They like to eat a little at a time, so feed them each time you water. Water them first. Several hours later, mix a little diluted water-soluble fertilizer (the kind packaged especially for African violets) and carefully pour it into the pot, from the top. Be sure not to drip or spill on the leaves or crown.

Temperature and Humidity

It would seem that African violets were made for the fuel crisis. They love temperatures of 60°F at night and 70°F during the day. If the temperature gets too high, buds will fall; if too low, foilage starts to curl and growth slows. Relative humidity of 50 percent is preferred and encourages them to bloom at their best.

Propagation

One of the best ways to get more plants from the African violets you have is by leaf propagation. It's simple, clean and quite reliable. Cut healthy leaves with inch-long stems from the parent plant using a very sharp knife or single-edge razor blade. Cut the bottom of the stem on an angle so there is more open area for rooting.

To root in water, place aluminum foil or waxed paper over the top of a small jar or bottle filled with warm water. Insert the leaf stems through holes in the covering, making sure the stem is in the water. To root in a pot, insert the stems into potting soil, vermiculite or either of the two mixed with peat moss. Insert a few ice cream sticks around the edge of the pot and cover pot, plant and sticks with clear plastic. You can expect your first beautiful African violet blooms about eight months after putting the leaves in for rooting.

try it

MINIATURE ROSES

Miniature roses, also called fairy roses, are something extra special. Perfect duplicates, in every detail, of the normal-sized hybrid tea roses, they have the same shaped dark-green leaves, same perfectly shaped bud and flower and even the same thorns. These beauties never grow taller than 18 inches and give you the same wide range of colors as tea roses: white, orange, yellow, red, pink and more. Cinderella, Starina and Bo-Peep are some varieties of miniature roses you might consider for your greenhouse. When selecting your plants, decide to buy the best and consider the color you prefer, the height of the mature plant, the amount of fragrance, and the density of thorns.

The miniature roses bought from a mail-order nursery come through the mail packed bare root. Open the package immediately and place the plants in a pail containing water and one-fourth the recommended (on the bag) amount of fertilizer. Submerge only the roots in water, keeping the stems and leaves dry. Leave in water 12 to 24 hours depending upon the plants' state of "dryness" when they arrived.

Pot the roses in clay pots, choosing a size that allows an extra one-half inch of soil around the roots when they are spread out. Pot in a mixture of three parts potting soil or humus, two parts peat moss and one part coarse sand. Moisten the soil and shape it into an inverted cone about four inches high in the bottom of the pot. Set the rose bush on top of the cone and drape the roots down the sides. Fill the pot with soil mixture and water thoroughly.

Miniature roses like sun (at least four hours a day) and fresh, circulating air. The temperature that keeps them happiest and blooming most profusely is between 50° and 60°F. They will do all right at 70°F, but will suffer if the temperature goes higher.

Miniature roses love water, not only in their soil, but in their air, which is why they are so perfect for a greenhouse. Water thoroughly when the soil begins to feel a bit dry to the touch. Don't wait too long or they'll drop their leaves. Feed only once a month and in small amounts. By late May or June the roses can be set outdoors to grace a window box, patio, garden or path.

Prune them as you would normal-sized rose bushes: carefully and gently, using very sharp clippers. Remove dead buds, poorly growing branches and stems going in strange directions to keep the plant healthy and looking its best.

If you give miniature roses the little bit of extra care and attention they need, they will give you a great deal of pleasure in the greenhouse, in your home and outdoors for many years.

GREENHOUSE CUTTING GARDEN

One of the many joys of your greenhouse is that it allows you to grow and enjoy a wide variety of beautiful, flowering, potted plants. You watch them mature and develop and, when they reach their peak of perfection, bring them into your home to brighten both your home and your heart.

As for "cut" flowers, they were always considered a luxury only the very rich could afford. Now your greenhouse allows you the same luxury. Set aside a portion of your greenhouse especially for flowers that can be cut and arranged for display in your home. There really is nothing to compare with the sight and scent of fresh flowers. Here are some you should try, all of which can easily be started from seed. As a matter of fact, this time we'll say, try them . . . you'll love them.

Ageratum

It's hard to sing the blues when talking about flowers, but finding blue flowers is quite difficult. Here's a pretty one in various shades of blue. Plant in light, sandy soil, give steady moisture and lots of sunlight. Feed with diluted fertilizer every other week. Try some of the taller growing varieties; they look more impressive in arrangements. Night temperatures around 55°F are best.

try it

Aster *(Callistephus)*

These can be grown all year long for flowers all year long. Lots of sunlight and a bit of shade in the hottest weather and you'll have wonderful flowers to cut. Decide which you prefer—single-stemmed flowers or bunches. Pinching gives more flowers per plant; single-stemmed flowers are larger. Either way they will need some support; use wire or string to keep them standing erect. Plant in quick-draining soil (extra sand) and water frequently. Feed only once from seed to flower. Keep night temperatures at about 50°F.

Carnation *(Dianthus)*

What is there to say about these great favorites that you don't already know? Great for corsages, boutonnières and arrangements (even one in a small vase is perfect), you can plant them in various colors including red, pink and white. White is fun, because by adding food coloring to the water you can create fascinating effects.

Plant in rich soil loaded with organic material. Keep night temperatures about 50°F. Add moisture sparingly as these plants do not like to stand in too-moist soil. Give full sun but protect against extremely high heat. Feed monthly. Use supports for these tall growers or they will fall over. For the largest flowers, pinch off buds, leaving only one bud on each stalk.

Lupine *(Lupinus)*

Start these from seed and plan to leave them right where they are because they do not transplant well. Sow in soil with good drainage. Water sparingly and only when soil is dry to the touch. Feed monthly and keep in night temperatures around 55°F. These plants also grow tall and need support.

Marigold *(Tagetes)*

Everyone knows of these plants, yet few grow them in the greenhouse. They will do beautifully in this controlled environment and supply many colorful, long-lasting cut flowers. Good rich soil, ample water and frequent feeding bring out the best in these favorites. Sunlight during the day and 50°F temperatures at night are tickets to success. And an added dividend, some of the "smellier" varieties keep bugs away from other plants.

Snapdragon *(Antirrhinum)*

You must try these because they are fascinating to see, easy to grow and produce a plethora of wonderful cut flowers. Plant only in sterilized soil to reduce the chance of rot taking hold. Give plenty of sun all year long but shade a bit during hottest summer months. Water frequently and maintain night temperatures in the 50°F range. Keep stems straight on supports and cut stems carefully as they flower to assure continuous blooms over a long period of time. Be sure to select those varieties bred especially for growing indoors.

Stock *(Mathiola)*

Color and fragrance make these special favorites with greenhouse gardeners. Plant in rich soil with extra peat moss added that is kept dry in winter and a bit wetter during the warm months. Once seedlings are up, feed with diluted fertilizer every other week. Keep in a spot that gets good ventilation, lots of sun, but not too many drafts. Night temperatures must not rise above 55°F. Use supports to keep plants growing upright.

Zinnia

Try these and you'll get more than you bargained for—more color that is. Plant in soil enriched with organic matter that has extra sand to help drainage. Keep the plants where they'll get plenty of sunlight and fresh air. Water only after soil feels quite dry and feed twice each month. Night temperatures of about 60°F are best. When in bloom, they are so lovely they almost beg to be cut and "arranged."

winning against bugs and diseases

WARNING!!
THIS GREENHOUSE
OFF LIMITS
TO BUGS

OK. Outdoors we're willing to fight them. After all, it is their land and we are the intruders. So in the garden, when the insects and the diseases and aggravation they cause descend, we shrug and make ready to fight.

But in our very own greenhouse, it is not easy to be quite as philosophical. Here we are resentful, despite all that talk about the balance of nature. When some blankety-blank, six-legged creature is wreaking havoc among our beautiful plants or tiny larvae are sucking the juice and life out of our vegetables, reason flies out the louvers and war is declared.

We feel the best thing is not to have any bugs in the first place. There are all sorts of preventive maintenance measures to insure, as much as possible, little if any insect problem in the greenhouse.

Keep it clean. No, that's not necessarily the "thought for the day," nor are we telling you how to think and live. Cleanliness is, however, the best preventive medicine for your greenhouse. The following good housekeeping practices are the first and most important steps in avoiding an insect and disease problem.

• Buy your plants only from reputable nurseries. Inspect your plants and their pots very carefully before you bring them into the greenhouse. Even plants that you bring in from outdoors, after the summer, must be carefully checked. Don't be too nice to friends or neighbors. When requested to be a plant sitter (for vacationing friends) or a plant doctor ("because you have a greenhouse," or "you're so good with plants"), learn to say no, or at least be alert and cautious before bringing "strangers" into your clean atmosphere.

• Use your eyes. Watch and check your plants, constantly searching for signs of problems—insects or diseases. If you spot something early, it is that much easier to correct. Learn the symptoms of disease: spotting, wilting, color changes, holes, powdery deposits, curling or browning on the leaves and stunted growth of the entire plant. Don't only look at the tops of leaves; many insects deposit their eggs on the undersides.

• If you find a badly diseased or infested plant, the best solution is to get rid of it. Get it out of the greenhouse *fast* before it has a chance to infect anything else. Most of us don't have another place to keep sick plants so the best idea is to get rid of them. And, get rid of everything —plant, soil and pot. There is always the possibility that the organisms are so well entrenched in the clay that even sterilizing may not kill those which have grown into the pores. Considering the widespread havoc which might be caused and the small cost of a new pot, throw everything out and start fresh.

• Keep the area surrounding your greenhouse as neat and clean as the inside. Throwing diseased plants or parts of plants onto a heap outside the greenhouse door is totally worthless. The wind and your shoes will carry the disease right back inside. Pull up all weeds and keep the area clean at all times.

• Keep a supply of plastic bags in the greenhouse. Make it a practice, once a week, to go over all plants. Remove dead or dying leaves, old stems and anything else that doesn't belong there. Put the garbage in a plastic bag, seal the bag, and on your way back to the house drop it directly into the garbage can.

bugs and diseases

- Use sterilized seed-starting mixtures. Such soilless products cut down on problems which can be introduced through the soil.
- Fresh air is a great way to keep disease problems to a minimum. Make sure your fans, louvers and vents are accessible and working.
- Last, but certainly not least, keep your plants as strong and healthy as you possibly can. The hardier your plants are, the better will be their resistance to disease. Select, as often as possible, disease-resistant varieties rather than give insects and diseases an easy variety to attack.

There is a philosophy which advocates regular, periodical, general spraying or fumigating of your greenhouse. *We do not agree with nor subscribe to this practice.* However, for those who insist on spraying, we mention it here.

Monthly sprayings are suggested and a variety of insecticides, pesticides and fungicides are available for such purposes. Always follow manufacturer's directions carefully, leave the greenhouse as soon as possible after spraying and bathe immediately. Also, wash the clothes you wear when spraying before wearing them again. To repeat, we don't like this method, we don't do it, and so we don't advocate it.

We prefer to find a solution to a problem only when we have a problem. Careful watching will bring a problem to your attention very soon after its onset. Determine what the cause is and set about finding the right solution; apply it and you should achieve success quickly and easily. This is, we feel, the better way.

DISEASES IN THE GREENHOUSE

Problems in the greenhouse can be caused by insects or diseases. Diseases are caused by viruses, bacteria and fungi. They are infectious and exasperating to all greenhouse gardeners because when symptoms appear, it's too late and the damage has been done.

Viruses live and reproduce in the body of the plant. Because of this, insects that feed on that plant transmit the disease to other plants as they move about. Viral diseases are systemic, infecting and infesting an entire plant. Plants which have viral diseases must be destroyed and discarded. Removing what you think to be an infected leaf or stem will not help at all. Obviously, control of insects in the greenhouse will also control possible spread of viral infections.

Bacteria are also tiny organisms, though not as tiny as viruses, and they also cause plant disease. Although some bacteria will attack more than one type of plant, most bacteria species will infect only "their own" specific host. Because they are not systemic parasites, a plant which has been attacked by a bacterial infection need not be discarded but may be "doctored" by removing the infected leaves or branches.

"There's a fungus among us," is not funny when applied to the plants in your greenhouse. Fungi are produced by spores, microscopic in size and impossible to detect until they are well established and it's too late. The tiny spore burrows its way into the plant through any opening it can find, natural or otherwise, and once in there, can't be reached by anything sprayed on the outer surface. This is one area in which preventive spraying might be a good idea. The residue of the spray, left on the outer parts of the plant, will kill any spores which come to visit and never give them a chance to settle in and stay to cause infection and grief. You should discard those plants infected by fungi.

BUGS AND MORE BUGS

Then there are the greenhouse insects. We suspect their sole function in this world is to turn us innocent, fun-loving greenhouse gardeners into raving maniacs. These threats to serenity and sanity come in three varieties: chewing (such as cutworms, leaf rollers), suckers (aphids, white flies, red spiders), and raspers (thrips).

Ants: Though we tend to think of them as harmless because they do no damage themselves, they truly do cause grief. Ants tend to move aphids from plant to plant, causing the spread of an aphid infestation.

Aphids: Also called plant lice, they may be yellow, greenish, black or white. They are small in size with plump bodies (that's from stuffing themselves on our magnificent plants). Some grow wings when food supplies become short, enabling them to fly to another food source.

bugs and diseases

Beetles: Not all are harmful and not all will enter the greenhouse. However the flea beetle (very small, black or metallic in color with horizontal stripes) will eat holes in primroses and stock. Blister beetles (long and narrow, occasionally striped) will munch on the flowers of the aster, gladioli and phlox.

Gnats: The larvae are called maggots and are yellowish-white with black heads. The maggots usually work underground, feeding on roots of almost any plant. The adults are suckers and are slender and black.

Leaf hoppers: These triangular-shaped, greenish-gray insects are about one-eighth to one-fourth inch in length. They enjoy your asters and chrysanthemums.

Leaf miners: These larvae are also known as maggots and their damage is to leaves. A look at the underside of an infected leaf will reveal brownish, twisting trails. These leaves should be removed and burned. Leaf miners attack asters, carnations, chrysanthemums, columbines and delphiniums.

Leaf rollers: These pests are caterpillars of green or bronze. They cause the leaves to roll up, then they build their cozy webbed nests inside and privately, undisturbed, proceed to feed on the leaf. Asters, carnations, geraniums, snapdragons and sweet peas are susceptible to leaf roller attack.

Leaf tiers: This is another caterpillar, similar in color and style to the leaf roller. The tier spins its web on the underside of a leaf and there, hidden, feeds at its leisure. Carnations, chrysanthemums, anemones and calceolarias are vulnerable to this pest.

Mealy bugs: When young, these nuisances are cottony looking. Adults are one-fifth to one-third of an inch in length with hairy-looking, waxy-coated projections. They are suckers and cause tremendous damage to African violets, begonias, chrysanthemums, gardenias, geraniums, poinsettias and orchids.

Midges: The larvae are maggots, one-half inch long and white. Although there are several types of midges, they all produce the same effect—galls, lumpy knobs ultimately causing deformity and warped growth. Galls may simply be cut off and burned. Chrysanthemums are susceptible to midge attack.

Mites: These are true members of the spider family and have eight legs to prove it. They are sucking pests and cause deformity and curling of the leaves, weak twisted plants, "rusting" of the leaves, and shriveling of flower buds. The red spider mite attacks asters, calceolarias, carnations chrysanthemums, gardenias, gladioli, lantanas, orchids, roses and sweet peas.

Nematodes: These are tiny roundworms that can attack roots and produce galls. Plants then become stunted and deformed. African violets, begonias and chrysanthemums are affected. As the nematodes live in the soil, steam sterilization is a very effective control but should be done by professionals. There is another nematode that attacks the foliage, leaving distinct brown spots. This is a clear case in which wetting the foliage will make the problem worse.

Scale: A small white or brown sucking insect with a round or oval top. One type sucks out juices and then injects a poison back into the host plant. The other type exudes a liquid on which sooty mildew grows. They are easily visible and some may be picked off or squashed. They attack ferns, palms, poinsettias, ivies, cacti and more.

Slugs and snails: Not a vaudeville team nor an advertising agency, and above all, not welcome in your greenhouse. Slugs and snails love humidity and moisture, so what better place for them to take up residence? They are easy to spot if you are looking for evidence that they are there. They leave a slimy mucus trail, large ugly holes in leaves, flowers, bulbs and fruit and produce eggs in watery clusters of 20 to 100. These eggs can hatch in from 10 days (under the most favorable conditions) to 100 days.

Their hundreds and hundreds of teeth are what do the job on your plants. They love dark, damp spots and spend their days there, coming out to feed at night. Be especially careful you don't bring them into the greenhouse on pots and plants from outdoors. Check and double check everything brought into the greenhouse after summering outside.

bugs and diseases

If you discover the presence of slugs and snails, try a few "home remedies." A small, flat saucer of beer attracts them. They happily crawl in and drown. Hunt for them at night with a flashlight and sprinkle salt on those you find. It sounds awful, but it dissolves them. They can't crawl over sandy, gritty substances, so sprinkle gravel, wood or coal ashes, sand or lime around plants. And, of course, try not to have any moist, dark spots for them to call home.

Sowbugs and pillbugs: Sowbugs and pillbugs love damp, protected places. What better place for them than your greenhouse? These insects love to hide under boards or flower pots. They have flat, oval, grayish bodies and are about one-half inch long. The pillbug is the one that curls up into a ball. They'll feed on your sweet peas, carnations, orchids, pansies, cinerarias as well as other flowers.

Thrips: These are the raspers and are injurious to flowers, foliage and fruit. They are very tiny insects, barely visible to the naked eye. Because they are so small, they are often not detected until the damage has been done. Their damage is revealed by white spots on stems and upper surfaces of leaves, leaves wilting and dying, and fruit or foliage spotted with black.

White flies: These are frequently found in greenhouses and are real nuisances, but controlling them is possible. They rest on the undersides of the leaves, and you might not even notice their presence unless the plant is disturbed. Then they fly up, looking like a white snowy puff. White flies cause foliage discoloration and also secrete a "honeydew" profusely. They enjoy dining on begonias, cinerarias, geraniums, fuchsias and snapdragons.

Now, before tearing up your greenhouse order, demolishing the one you already have or cursing the day you even considered getting one, let us assure you that not only will you not have all these problems, you will also not have most of them. You will probably, after a while, be stuck with a couple of them, but they are easily eliminated, so don't give it more emphasis in your mind than is absolutely necessary.

SOME PROBLEM SOLVING

As we said at the beginning of this chapter, the best thing you can do to avoid a bug invasion is to practice preventive maintenance. That will take care of most problems. The rest can also be solved.

Another useful but after-the-fact method of controlling insects is to plant certain crops in your greenhouse which repel insects. Organic gardeners have advocated companion planting, outdoors, for years. It works indoors, too. Mint and marigolds, onions, garlic and chives, rosemary, rue, tansy and thyme work wonders.

If you grow a number of pots or flats of one variety, don't set them all together in one section of the greenhouse. Scatter them around as much as possible, preferably next to completely different types of plants. In this way, should an insect harmful to one plant get started, he can't feast right down the line for a full meal.

You could also adopt a friendly local toad or a chameleon and let it live in your greenhouse; they eat insects. Plant praying mantis cases and let them hatch, or buy ladybugs, lacewings or trichogramma wasps and turn them loose to "do their thing."

Devise and develop your own homemade, natural sprays and repellents. Here are some recommended by many greenhouse gardeners.

• Any combination of onions, chives, mint, hot peppers, tobacco and horseradish. Put whatever you choose into your blender with some water and liquify. Strain and pour into a sprayer. Works wonders.

• Mix a tablespoon of dishwashing liquid in a gallon of water. Spray plant, soil and pot, and don't wash it off; it won't harm the plant.

• Yellow has been proven to attract white flies as well as aphids. Spray yellow index cards or larger pieces of cardboard painted yellow with a sticky substance and place them around the greenhouse.

• Often, liquifying the leaves of plants which are not affected by certain insects or diseases and spraying them on the affected ones will work wonders. (Liquify them in a blender.) Apparently, whatever makes them immune to attack can be transmitted by spraying.

• Make a nicotine spray by soaking cigar and cigarette butts in water.

winning
the bug war

If, after trying all the insect chasing and killing suggestions, you still have a problem, here are some solutions. To make it a bit easier, we have combined some natural remedies, some home remedies and some "last resort" remedies (asterisked) listed according to the bugs they control.

ANTS		*Malathion	
APHIDS		Lay a collar of foil around rim of pot; they are repelled by aluminum. Set out yellow saucer filled with	detergent water; they are attracted and drown. Nicotine, Pyrethrum, Rotenone, *Malathion
BEETLES		Rotenone, Pyrethrum, *Malathion	
GNATS		Protect bulbs by soaking them in hot water (110°) for 5 hours before planting.	Spray with tobacco juice.
LEAF HOPPERS		*Sevin, *Malathion	
LEAF MINERS		Hand pick leaves or infested portion of plant and burn. *Malathion	
LEAF ROLLERS		Hand pick infested leaves and burn. Pyrethrum, *Sevin, *Malathion	

Pest			Remedy	Remedy
MEALY BUGS			Tobacco spray Just a few can be killed by dabbing with cotton soaked in rubbing alcohol.	*Malathion (mix with a few drops of household detergent) *Sevin
MITES			Spray water on suspected areas of infestation. They like it dry—don't like moisture.	Dust with powdered sulphur.
MIDGE			Cut off galls and burn.	
NEMATODES			Steam sterilization of soil. Remove and destroy badly infested plants.	Keep foliage dry.
SCALE			Nicotine with soap If only a few, hand pick and burn.	Using soap and water, scrub with a small brush. *Malathion, *Sevin
SLUGS & SNAILS			Hand pick at night and destroy. Sprinkle salt on slugs.	Sprinkle ashes, sand, grit on the ground. Scatter lime on the ground.
SOW-BUGS			Trap under damp flower pots. *Malathion	
THRIPS			Spray with a mixture of garlic, onion juice, hot pepper and water.	Rotenone, Pyrethrum, *Malathion
WHITE FLIES			Use vacuum cleaner nozzle. Yellow cardboard sprayed with sticky substance.	Yellow saucers filled with detergent water; they're attracted, drown. *Malathion

greenhousing calendar

One of the most exciting advantages to having a greenhouse is being able to do just about anything at just about any time. The carefully controlled environment, including temperature, humidity and light, allows you to plant tomatoes in January, snapdragons in December and chives in March, to name just a very few.

Here as elsewhere though, it makes more sense to schedule certain tasks at certain times. If you can start tomatoes at any time, why not start them in the fall so you will be eating those tomatoes in January, not first planting them? If you want holiday plants for gifts, why start them in November when it will be just a little too late? Back up a little so they will be ready when you want and need them.

So, a greenhouse calendar. When to do the fun projects, when to do the mundane jobs and when to do the not-always-pleasant, but oh-so-necessary, chores. Add your own notes to our calendar or devise your own and it will help develop a rhythm, a pattern to your greenhousing, for getting things done, properly, at the right times for you.

Sunday	Monday	Tuesday	Wednesday	Thursday	Friday	Saturday

For us, in the greenhouse, this is the beginning of the new year, not January 1. We come back into the greenhouse "officially" after the full summer outdoors. This does not mean the greenhouse has been either empty or idle all summer, just that it has not taken our primary attention.

HOUSEKEEPING Remove everything from the greenhouse. Wash the glass, fiber glass or plastic inside. Make sure all panels are perfect, with no chips or cracks, and replace now, as required. Rake or sweep the floor. Wash down benches and tables. Empty and clean all large trays, watering cans, etc. outdoors before bringing them back into the greenhouse. Check the heater to make sure it is working properly. Check the fan and humidifier. Though the humidifier is not used now, make sure it works. If you have had any covering to provide shade for the greenhouse, remove it.

PREPARATION Buy, mix and be sure you have enough potting soil, compost, humus, peat moss, leaf mold, etc. Be sure you have pots, shards, label blanks, extra trays and proper tools for the coming year's activities.

FUN TO DO Decide what you will be bringing back into the greenhouse from the garden. Check and double check, before you bring them in, to be sure plants and pots are insect free. Use this month to start preparing for the Christmas and New Year holidays. If yours is a fresh vegetable-loving family, plant cauliflower now for perfect holiday eating or unusual, but often appreciated, giving. Investigate the world of miniature vegetables. Try Tiny Sweet Carrot (65 days) or Mini-Cucumber (55 days). Planting them about the 15th will put them on your Thanksgiving table. And, in just 60 days, you can be the proud parent of a mini-cantaloupe. The four-inch melons grow on compact vines which only reach about 22 inches across. Also select the flowers you'll want for your holiday table and for giving as gifts. Make cuttings of some of your own plants or plant some of those described in the chapter on blooming plants.

october

A must for this month, especially if you live in an area of very cold winters, is the purchase and installation of heavy-duty, clear plastic sheeting. No matter how well you think your greenhouse is sealed, it isn't perfect. If on a breezy day you place your hand in front of a joint, you'll soon see exactly how non-airtight your greenhouse is. When temperatures go down into the 20's and teens, you'll want your house closed against as much cold air as possible.

Buy enough sheeting to go completely around the inside of the house, including walls and ceiling. Cut the plastic into the largest size pieces you can possibly handle comfortably. Use heavy-duty tape to attach the sheeting to the metal or wooden supports. Don't press it tight against the windows; let the plastic hang away from the glass allowing for an air space. The air space will provide additional insulation and save more heat.

Cut an extra piece of sheeting and use it to make a large wide flap to tape over the doorway. Make sure the pieces that cover the walls extend about six inches below floor level. Bend the extra length inward so it can be covered with a layer of floor gravel, a brick or similar weight to seal the floor/wall gap. We'll remind you later in the calendar to mark the pieces of plastic and the supports when you take the plastic down. Then when it's time to rehang it in the fall next year, you'll know which piece was cut to fit where.

HOUSEKEEPING The heater will be operating now as many areas get heavy frost at night. If you have a humidifier or mister be sure it is in operation. If you don't, be sure there is plenty of water in the greenhouse so plants get the moisture they need. A large plastic garbage can filled with clean water will provide enough moisture through evaporation.

PREPARATION Start forcing bulbs this month. Check blooming dates, see what you want to have for yourself, and what you'd like to give as gifts. Then count backwards and determine the proper planting time.

FUN TO DO If you have poinsettias, do not expose them to any artificial light. They are forming their buds and will get crazy if they get too much or erratic light. Plant an assortment of herbs: Chives, sage, thyme, rosemary and others will add to the fun and productivity of your greenhouse. Take cuttings from coleus, lantana, shrimp plant and heliotrope if you have them and taking cuttings is your thing.

You'll be spending more time in your greenhouse, not by necessity, but by choice. As the weather gets colder and nastier outside, there's little that's nicer than retreating to your wonderful green oasis under glass. Be good to yourself. Get a cassette player or radio so you can enjoy lovely music while you enjoy your plants. If you had no lights before, bring in a lamp which will allow you to work during the evenings, now that it gets dark earlier.

HOUSEKEEPING Get four or five inexpensive thermometers. Place them at various spots in the greenhouse. Check the temperature in different locations. Cooler places will be better for certain plants, bulbs, etc. The thermometers will also tell you if cold air is finding its way into one particular spot and give you a chance to seal it out. Similarly, if something is blocking the warm air from certain spots, you can make arrangements to correct that situation.
Make sure you have emergency equipment should anything fail: extra heavy plastic if glass breaks, a supplementary heater if the heater malfunctions, etc.

PREPARATION This is the time to start watering certain plants and start withholding water from others. Either move them and group them according to water or no-water, or prepare labels reminding you. These labels will also be helpful to well-meaning friends or neighbors, if you take a winter vacation or have a sudden bout with the flu. Nothing is more confusing to a plant sitter than trying to figure out what to water and what not to water. Get and position stakes and supports for those plants that will need them.

FUN TO DO Find, make, invent or buy hangers for hanging planters. Simple macramé hangers can be made with three or four easy knots. Make it a family project and one evening's work should produce enough to last several years. Also, consider making or gathering the flats you'll need to start your vegetables under glass. Seeds which can be sown now for late spring and early summer bloom include candytuft, marigold (don't forget Burpee's new Pure White), petunia, sweet alyssum, sweet pea, nasturtium, snapdragon, larkspur. Try starting tuberous begonias and gloxinias from seed; you'll have flowers by summer.

december

With the holidays fast approaching and not enough time in each day to get everything ready, we'll take it easy in the greenhouse this month and not look for any big projects. We'll just enjoy it as a wonderful oasis where we can relax and let our minds drift for a couple of hours each week. Remember to water in the mornings and try to avoid getting water on leaves. There is less sun now and what there is, is not terribly strong; any water you use will be absorbed more slowly. Send for seed catalogs for your spring planting.

HOUSEKEEPING The greenhouse has been "in production" for a solid three months. Comparing it to your "other house," the one in which you live the rest of the time, you'll realize it's been a long time between house cleanings. Take a large plastic garbage bag out with you on your next visit. Cut, clip and prune plants that require grooming. Pick up leaves and generally tidy the benches, flats, pots and floor. If potting soil has spilled, sweep and dump. Rake gravel if necessary. Check plastic insulation sheeting to be sure it is in place.

FUN TO DO Day by day, little by little, start getting your holiday gift and house plants ready for their big day. Repot all those that seem to need it. Make, buy or otherwise find pretty pots, hanging holders and ways to most attractively wrap or display. Consider adding a useful mat to your gift package to be placed under the flower pot so the recipient doesn't have to look for one when the gift is presented. All he or she need do is unwrap, locate and enjoy.

Start bringing some of your blooming beauties into the house. They'll bring cheer and good feelings in right along with them. If you have school-age children, let them prepare and pot some cuttings for their friends and teachers to share and enjoy.

Sunday	Monday	Tuesday	Wednesday	Thursday	Friday	Saturday

This is a great month for relaxing and planning what the next two seasons will bring, both indoors and outdoors. Seed catalogs will arrive this month. Give yourself several days to go over them to see and compare what is offered and decide what you will use and enjoy most of all. Go back over your notes from the past year, reviewing your successes and failures, amount grown, amount eaten or canned and make decisions. To grow or not to grow. To can or not to can. To bother or not to bother. Remember to always select the varieties especially suited to your area. And, if space is at a premium (either in the greenhouse or, later, outdoors), plant only those vegetables and flowers your family likes best of all.

HOUSEKEEPING Depending upon where you live, this may be snow time. Try to keep snow off the roof of your greenhouse. If there is a big storm, you may have to use a heavy-duty broom to remove the snow. Watch that ice does not stick. Keep a close eye on the areas around vents or louvers and keep these ice-free. If your heater vents outside, keep that ice-free, too.
Snow weather is nasty cold weather. The heater will be "on" more often and for longer periods. Because of this, you'll need to watch the moisture level in the greenhouse. Watering more often, extra pans of water, dampening down walkways or gravel are all ways to increase the moisture and humidity levels.

FUN TO DO Consider making a little pin money from your efforts. Many greenhouse owners have discovered that there is a market for their products. If this thought has crossed your mind, this is the time to start candytuft, larkspur, stock, petunia. All will be mature, flowering and ready to sell in May. Also, in mid-January you can pot begonias (all kinds, including tuberous), gloxinia, calla lily, caladium and amaryllis bulbs. They too will mature and flower in May.

177

february

What a great month for a greenhouse. What a great way to lick the winter doldrums. No matter where you are there seems to be nasty weather, colds and flu. To go out into the greenhouse is truly an escape to another world. Housekeeping chores are minimal. By now all equipment should be working and plants should be moving along at their own rate of speed, doing whatever it is they are supposed to do. Remember planting, potting and repotting time is fast approaching. Make doubly sure you have all the supplies you'll need.

FUN TO DO For early June flowering indoors, you can now sow China aster, snapdragon, ageratum, stock, petunia and alyssum. They need warmth (70° to 80°F). *Celosia*, coleus and *Gypsophila* are very beautiful foliage plants and can be started now for mature plants in June.

March is exciting, not only because there is so much to do in the greenhouse, but also because there are hints of spring in the air. Outdoors, crocuses and tulips pop suddenly into view, pussy willow buds fatten and explode, and spring fever creeps into your bones and makes you itchy for "the great outdoors" once again.

HOUSEKEEPING With warm days and chilly days alternating to confuse you, your plants and your heating system, make sure your greenhouse ventilating system is working well. Be certain the vent is clear and operating well, because you'll find it working to open and cool your greenhouse more often than you'd expect.

april

Spring is finally here—temporarily at least. In April, the sun is warmer, the days are longer and we begin to think the worst is behind us. In our part of the country this condition usually lasts several weeks and then we find ourselves in the midst of a heat spell that is more like summer than spring. But, for now, it is spring.

HOUSEKEEPING Once the danger of freezing temperatures is over, remove plastic insulation. Remember to number the pieces and their supports so you can reconstruct them in October. Shade is the biggest and most important item on the housekeeping agenda this month. Make sure you provide it, however you prefer, for all the plants that will need it in your greenhouse. Also check the temperature at which your vent thermostat has been set all winter. You might want to consider changing it (about 10 degrees above the heat thermostat is good) now that the weather has warmed. Give all your plants a good spritzing of liquid detergent and water (about one tablespoon per gallon of water). This is a wonderful and a safe way to keep down the problem of white fly and many other insects. It doesn't harm the plants but makes the bugs miserable. Spray thoroughly, top and bottom sides of leaves, blooms, stems and soil.

FUN TO DO What could possibly be more fun and satisfying than to start your vegetable and flower seedlings for later transplanting into your outdoor garden? Remember that flower seeds, as compared to seedlings, tubers, etc., are very inexpensive. For your summer cutting garden, now is the time to sow seeds for asters, snapdragons, marigolds, cosmos, ageratum, petunias, *Celosia* and statice. Start morning glory seeds for your summer outdoor garden. Something you might not have realized is that each seed will not be exactly the same as all the others in a package, and there might be quite a surprise when blooming time comes.
Mother's Day is next month. Prepare cuttings, transplant seedlings, repot and make attractive gifts for giving or for selling. If you can bring yourself to do it, cut off a branch or two of your forsythia bush and force it into bloom indoors by placing it in a bucket of water. Decide what bulbs you'd like to have on hand for forcing next winter; order now. Hyacinths, daffodils, tulips, paper whites and freesias are excellent choices.

may

Here the babies go out of the greenhouse and into the ground. The vegetable and flower seedlings we have watched and nurtured so carefully all these weeks go into the cold frame for hardening off, then into the garden. By mid-May, you should be sure enough of the weather that even the tomatoes can be transplanted.

HOUSEKEEPING If you expect to continue using the greenhouse through the remainder of spring and summer, be sure it will be well shaded. Wet down the walks and gravel to cool the greenhouse during the warm weather.

PREPARATION This is your last chance to order bulbs for forcing next winter. Local nursery shelves are crammed full of all sorts of equipment and supplies. Remember not everyone is as lucky as we greenhouse owners are and can continue gardening all year. Local stores stock for the majority of buyers and that's *now*. Check your supplies and fill in whatever you need. Now is also the time to cut back your Christmas poinsettias and other winter bloomers. Cut back the original stem to between six and 12 inches. Water thoroughly when soil becomes dry to the touch. You may repot if you wish.

Plan your greenhouse budget for the coming year. Check your fuel bills for the "bad" winter months last year. Estimate as closely as possible the cost of running your greenhouse at your temperature. You may discover you have not spent as much as you thought and could afford to raise the temperature (and grow slightly warmer weather plants). Or you might say "*Wow*, what bills," and lower the setting for next year, still giving you the chance to experiment with a whole new assortment of plants.

FUN TO DO May is a good time to start flower seeds for fall bloom. While you are busy outdoors all summer, they will be growing and will suddenly surprise you next fall with a beautiful show. Consider sweet alyssum, wax begonia, browallia, China aster, Christmas pepper or cornflower.

june

Most of your concentration and time will be focused on the outdoors this month. Not much action is taking place in the greenhouse right now. It will be the rare gardener who doesn't have some outdoor area, small or large, in which to spend the summer months. Be sure your greenhouse is covered for the hot months to come. If any plants are left in the greenhouse, be sure they are fully shaded and all vents and louvers are in tip-top working order. Otherwise you may come home one day to find your plants cooked. Also continue to hose down walks and benches to keep the greenhouse cool and humidity up. Spray-mist plants often for the same reason.

HOUSEKEEPING If you are "closing up shop" in the greenhouse for the summer, remove everything and hose down the walls and floor. Check out heating and wiring systems as well as heating cables. Have repairs or replacements made now. If you are planning to replace bench soil, now is the best time to do it. Sterilize soil before it is in place. If there are any weeds in the floor, remove them. Clean pots and other equipment before returning them to the greenhouse.

PREPARATION Plan ahead: What will you be growing next winter? Now you have the time to go back over what you have done and think about your successes and failures. What might you do that you didn't do in the past? What could or would you do differently? Check supplies for your new requirements and order or buy what you'll need now, when stores and nurseries are well stocked.

FUN TO DO Start seeds now so your garden will continue growing through those long fall and winter months ahead. Two very beautiful flowers to try are heliotrope, with its heavily-scented flowers of purple, lavender, white or blue, or forget-me-nots, those very special blue beauties. Consider also *Kalanchoe* (pronounced kal-en-co-ee); choose from scarlet, yellow, purple, salmon or pink blooms. Another interesting and fragrant flower with a funny name is flowering tobacco *(Nicotiana),* which can be had in maroon, white or yellow-green.

This is a quiet time in the greenhouse. If you still have plants in it, be sure your ventilating system is working well and hose down walks and gravel to keep the humidity level up. You'll find your primary area of enthusiasm is outdoors now, so plan to do very little in the greenhouse. You won't do it anyway, so why plan a lot and feel guilty?

FUN TO DO Talk yourself into it. With tomatoes ripening constantly in the garden, the last thing on your mind is planting more tomatoes. But plant them you must, if you want to enjoy them next winter. Select a dwarf or mini-variety and plant now. Seeds will sprout happily at 75° to 80°F. Repot when true leaves appear, water well and feed every two to three weeks. Hand-pollinate when flowers open and you'll be glad you talked yourself into doing this in July when you start picking your red, ripe beauties next winter.

august

It is *hot, hot, hot*. We would rather do almost anything than go out in that broiling sun to garden. Going into the greenhouse isn't too tempting an idea either. Fortunately there isn't much happening in the greenhouse right now that would need our attention. As for the outdoor stuff, we take care of that early in the morning. Because it gets light so early every morning, we do our gardening at about six a.m. The sun is rosy and gorgeous, the air is cool, clean and clear, the grass and leaves are still wet with dew. It's absolutely quiet except for the songs of the birds—a magic time. We work for about a half to three-quarters of an hour and then relax with a light, "continental" breakfast in the shade of the patio. All in all, we feel very rich.

PREPARATION Now that the year has passed, are you pleased with what you had and did in your greenhouse? This will be a good time to make any changes you'd like to try. Also, at this time, you may find some new bulb and seed catalogs starting to arrive in the mail. This is the perfect opportunity to find your favorite shady spot, relax and "see what's new" for next year.

FUN TO DO First, have you considered putting a small but comfortable chair into a corner of your greenhouse? If your experience from last year suggests you might have even the tiniest amount of time to enjoy such comfort, do it. Although "working" in the greenhouse is relaxation and pleasure enough, that chair will allow you even more. Like many other "good" things, it's easy to get used to once you've given yourself the chance to try it. Geraniums, which probably have been thriving and growing like crazy outdoors all summer, can now be used to make additional plants. Take cuttings from poinsettias also. Sow seeds of calendula (to bloom in late December through March), stock (to bloom in January) or aster (to bloom in February and early March). Freesia corms potted now will bloom next May.

sources for greenhouse gardeners

GREENHOUSES AND ACCESSORIES

Aluminum Greenhouses, Inc.
14615 Lorain Avenue
Cleveland, Ohio 44111

Garden of Eden Greenhouses
875 E. Jericho Turnpike
Huntington Station, New York
    11746

George J. Ball, Inc.
(Greenhouse Accessories)
West Chicago, Illinois 60185

Janco Greenhouses
10788 Tucker Street
Beltsville, Maryland 20705

Lord and Burnham
(Greenhouses)
Irvington, New York 10533
    also
Des Plains, Illinois 60018

Peter Reumuller
(Greenhouses)
P.O. Box 2666
Santa Cruz, California 95060

Redfern's Prefab Greenhouses
55 Mt. Hermon Road
Scotts Valley, California 95060

Sudbury Laboratory, Inc.
(Soil Testing Equipment)
Box 1028
Sudbury, Massachusetts 01776

Turner Greenhouses
P.O. Box 1260
Goldsboro, North Carolina 27530

Vegetable Factory Greenhouses
P.O. Box 2235
Grand Central Station
New York, New York 10017

Walter F. Nicke
(Greenhouse Accessories)
P.O. Box 71
Hudson, New York 12534

SEEDS, PLANTS AND OTHER MATERIALS

Alberts & Merkel
(Ferns)
2210 S. Federal Highway
Boynton Beach, Florida 33435

Antonelli Brothers
2545 Capitola Road
Santa Cruz, California 95010

Arthur Freed Orchids
5731 S. Bonsall Drive
Malibu, California 90265

Buell's Greenhouses
(African Violets)
Weeks Road
Eastford, Connecticut 06242

Burgess Seed Company
Galesburg, Michigan 49053

Cactus Pete's
5454 Valley Boulevard
Los Angeles, California

Dean Foster Nurseries
Hartford, Michigan 49057

Edelweiss Gardens
Robbinsville, New Jersey 08691

Fennell Orchid Company
The Orchid Jungle
26715 S.W. 157 Avenue
Homestead, Florida 33030

sources

Fiser Greenhouses
(African Violets)
Linwood, New Jersey 08221

Floralite
(Supplies)
4124 E. Oakwood Road
Oak Creek, Wisconsin 53154

Geiger Orchids
P.O. Box 245
Welbourn, Florida 32094

George Park Seed Company
Greenwood, South Carolina
    29646

Hausermann's
(Orchids)
P.O. Box 363
Elmhurst, Illinois 60128

Henry Field Seed Company
Shenandoah, Iowa 51601

John Scheepers, Inc.
(Bulbs)
37 Wall Street
New York, New York 10005

John's Dewkist Nurseries
P.O. Drawer AC
Apopka, Florida 32703

Joseph Harris Company, Inc.
Moreton Farm
Buffalo Road
Rochester, New York 14624

Margaret Ilgenfritz
(Orchids)
P.O. Box 665
Monroe, Michigan 48161

Moore Miniature Roses
2519 E. Noble Avenue
Visalia, California 93277

Oregon Bulb Farms
Gresham, Oregon 97030

P. de Jager & Sons
(Bulbs)
188 Asbury Street
South Hamilton, Maine 01982

Putney Nursery
(Ferns)
Putney, Vermont 05346

Stern's Nurseries, Inc.
Geneva, New York 14456

Thompson & Morgan
401 Kennedy Boulevard
Somerdale, New Jersey 08083

Van Bourgondien's
(Bulbs)
245 Farmingdale Road
R. 109, Box A
Babylon, New York 11702

Violets by Elizabeth
3131 Montrose Avenue
Rockford, Illinois 61103

Volkmann Brothers
(Greenhouses)
2714 Minert Street
Dallas, Texas 75219

W. Atlee Burpee
300 Park Avenue
Warminster, Pennsylvania 18991

Walter Nicke
(Supplies)
Box 667
Hudson, New York 12534

Wayside Gardens
Hodges, South Carolina 29695

index

index

index

biographical data

ABOUT THE AUTHOR

DX Fenten is known to Long Island readers as "The Weekend Gardener" in the Sunday Magazine section of *Newsday*. This popular column was named the best newspaper gardening series in 1975 by the Women's National Farm & Garden Association, and recently published as a book. He is also the author of 22 other books, nine of them on the subject of gardening, and with his wife, Barbara, has co-authored two books on organic foods. The Fentens and their two teenage children live on Long Island amid gardens filled with organically raised flowers, fruits and vegetables and, of course, a greenhouse. Born and raised in New York City, DX Fenten received his B.A. and M.A. degrees from New York University. He serves as consultant to seed and nursery companies.

ABOUT THE ARTIST

Maggie Baylis is the author and illustrator of two best-selling books, *House Plants for the Purple Thumb* and *Practicing Plant Parenthood*. After studying architecture in college, she was for a number of years the assistant art director for *Sunset* magazine. Then for some 20 years she worked with her husband, the late Douglas Baylis, nationally known landscape architect, as draftsman and delineator, as well as consultants for the nation's leading home and garden publications. She has recently installed a small city greenhouse on the deck of her plant-filled studio/home on San Francisco's Telegraph Hill.

ABOUT THE ARCHITECT

Roy Killeen received his bachelor in architecture from Washington University in St. Louis, where he was an associate of the architectural firm William B. Ittner for a number of years. In 1960, he moved to San Francisco as project architect for Anshen and Allen and was responsible for several award-winning buildings. In 1968, Mr. Killeen co-founded the publishing firm of 101 Productions. He has designed and illustrated a number of 101 books and created the popular "Mini-Mansion" series of architectural model kits.